INFINITE IMPACT

Abdalla Nasr

INFINITE IMPACT

Your practical leadership playbook for today's corporate world

Abdalla Nasr

INFINITE IMPACT
Copyright © 2023 Abdalla Nasr
First published in 2023

Print: 978-1-76124-133-8
E-book: 978-1-76124-135-2
Hardback: 978-1-76124-134-5

All rights reserved. No part of this book may be reproduced, stored in a retrieval system, or transmitted by any means (electronic, mechanical, photocopying, recording, or otherwise) without written permission from the author.

Because of the dynamic nature of the Internet, any web addresses or links contained in this book may have changed since publication and may no longer be valid. The information in this book is based on the author's experiences and opinions. The views expressed in this book are solely those of the author and do not necessarily reflect the views of the publisher; the publisher hereby disclaims any responsibility for them.

The author of this book does not dispense any form of medical, legal, financial, or technical advice either directly or indirectly. The intent of the author is solely to provide information of a general nature to help you in your quest for personal development and growth. In the event you use any of the information in this book, the author and the publisher assume no responsibility for your actions. If any form of expert assistance is required, the services of a competent professional should be sought.

Publishing information
Publishing and design facilitated by
Passionpreneur Publishing
A division of Passionpreneur Organization Pty Ltd
ABN: 48640637529

Melbourne, VIC | Australia
www.PassionpreneurPublishing.com

*To everyone who helped me in my journey,
to my family and friends,
to my partner, and
to those who hustle daily
against all obstacles to be better employees,
leaders, and, most importantly, humans.*

Contents

Introduction ix

INTROSPECTION 1
1. Navigating the digital era with emotional intelligence 4
2. Leading with authenticity 17
3. The inner battle—overcoming self-doubt and imposter syndrome 29
4. Becoming bulletproof 39

IMPACT 61
1. Common leadership challenges 63
2. Leadership in the digital era 73
3. Cultivating growth mindsets to unlock high-performance teams 83
4. Transforming culture, empowering teams 95

5. Navigating corporate politics with
   integrity and purpose   109
6. Embracing diversity, equity, and inclusion
   for a stronger future   123
7. Motivation and drive   135
8. Fostering psychological safety for team excellence   149
9. Leading a multi-generational workforce   155
10. Overcoming burnout and prioritizing wellness   167
11. Mastering remote leadership with impact
    and empathy   177

Conclusion   181
References   185
Author Bio   189

Introduction

Despite the success of *The Corporate* in 2021, I never imagined writing and publishing another book. But as time passed, I saw how rapidly our world was changing. In my role of offering support to managers and leaders across the globe, I have witnessed some people succeed while others struggle in this new corporate landscape. Technology and the new norms have brought leaders opportunities but also significant challenges.

This book is not about traditional leadership theories. It aims to provide a practical playbook for people managers and leaders in organizations to use in their daily lives. Drawing from my experiences and the experiences of top leaders around the world, I will share best practices that you can immediately apply in your daily lives.

Leadership is far from easy. Often, as leaders you find yourself in uncharted territory, facing unprecedented situations with little room for failure or learning in a safe space. You are expected to possess all the answers and make crucial decisions, even in times of great uncertainty. While you may tirelessly support and care for our team, it can sometimes feel like you don't receive that same level of support for yourself. Every step, every gesture, and every action you take is scrutinized and evaluated. You are expected to drive results and hypergrowth while embodying empathy, understanding, and compassion. From day one, you are committed to recognizing your team's efforts, even when your own may go unrecognized. And when faced with tough times and difficult decisions, such as layoffs, the burden falls on your shoulders to take ownership and lead those conversations, sometimes bidding farewell to individuals you have spent a significant amount of time with. I hope those around you can grasp the challenges you face, because the role of a leader is far from easy.

Is it worth it?

I believe it is, and not for the money and the perks that come with it. Leadership is an incredibly profound role if done for the right reasons. The position allows you to make an infinite impact. It goes beyond the professional realm and influences people's lives in various ways, causing a ripple effect. It goes even further in today's digital world. As a leader, you can influence people across geographies, functions, companies, and generations, leaving a legacy that will be long remembered.

Despite the difficulties, there are leaders who rise to the challenges and find inspiration in them. The more they face, the more energized and committed they become. Through my experiences, I have observed and learned from such leaders, striving to understand the reasons behind their resilience. I have also witnessed leaders who, despite facing hardships, have

INTRODUCTION

discovered a unique leadership style that aligns with their true selves, freeing them from the need to imitate others.

In addition to the usual trials of leadership, today's world presents us with a host of additional opportunities and obstacles: digital transformation, managing multi-generational teams, addressing stress and burnout, developing emotional intelligence (EI), fostering empathy, driving results and growth, embracing diversity, equity, and inclusion, managing constant change, motivating teams, navigating remote work challenges, overcoming self-doubt—the list is extensive. This book acknowledges the limitations of your time by providing a direct and concise approach to tackle these topics. You may read it as a story or select specific chapters based on the pressing challenges you encounter. Although I understand your time is precious, I recommend that you eventually explore every chapter to equip yourself for whatever lies ahead—as you will undoubtedly encounter these challenges and more on your leadership journey. I guarantee it.

INTROSPECTION

1

NAVIGATING THE DIGITAL ERA WITH EMOTIONAL INTELLIGENCE

Emotional intelligence, commonly referred to as EI or EQ, is an individual's capability to comprehend and respond to others' emotions and manage their own emotions as well, particularly in interpersonal relationships, including in the workplace. A socially intelligent leader who applies EI principles finds that communication flows better, and thus employees' satisfaction, performance, and longevity all rise. A leader's capacity to use their emotional resources to detect issues before they occur or worsen makes them an essential change agent, resulting in increased productivity and outcomes that meet organizational goals.

In addition, a leader's emotional intelligence should be flexible enough to navigate crisis-related leadership events successfully. In such situations, their ability to remain grounded, empathize, and communicate clearly without camouflaging vital commitments or radical change agendas requires practiced emotional decision-making expertise.

Leaders with emotional intelligence can foster healthy workplace relationships, inspiring ingenuity and cultivating trust among subordinates, surfacing soft skills such as empathy, adaptability, and creativity, and ultimately spelling exponential team growth.

Effective leadership in a modern workplace extends beyond technical and functional knowledge to rely heavily on emotional intelligence attributes that foster impactful connections with those you work with.

Components of EQ

As mentioned earlier, emotional intelligence describes how well an individual understands and manages their emotions, behaviors, and reactions to different stimuli. Research highlights five key components that make up emotional intelligence, each of which should be viewed and practiced as correlates in tandem with each other in effective EQ-based leadership.

The first component is **self-awareness**. This refers to a leader's capacity to understand and have reflective insights into their behaviors' impact on situations. Leaders who incorporate self-awareness principles in day-to-day activities have a greater opportunity to understand their impact on employees and the

5

environment in which they work, ultimately creating a healthier culture.

The second component is **self-regulation** or **self-management**. This is the ability of an individual to manage their emotions and impulses in ways that foster their goals. When you learn to manage aimless emotional outbursts, you can achieve better impulse control with greater ease, set secure and focused objectives, and deliver tactful policies, practices, and decisions under high-pressure conditions. This is easier said than done. Many of us experience events that trigger something called an **amygdala hijack**—instead of processing information through our prefrontal cortex, the part of the brain responsible for reasoning and logic, the amygdala, a primitive part of the brain in the limbic region, is hijacked by intense emotions that cause us to react irrationally and do things we mostly regret later.

Third, **empathy** is another essential component of emotional intelligence. Leaders who direct empathetic gestures toward others, such as genuineness and active listening, facilitate lasting relationships in the workplace, making it a place where colleagues want to succeed collectively. This leads to further collaboration, less dissonance, and measurable increases in team productivity. Empathy alone is a large topic. It is very difficult to be a leader that people will choose to follow if you lack empathy.

The fourth component of emotional intelligence is **social skills**. These competencies integrate with communication patterns, teamwork, and effective communication to find common ground at work and create teammate-focused initiatives, affecting the collaborative force by providing solutions and feedback. Leaders with striking social skills tend to find efficient ways to transform goals among employees, both on smaller and larger scales.

Finally, **motivation** is the fifth component famously associated with emotional intelligence. We will discuss motivation in depth later in the book. Motivation is the capacity to set and pursue goals, have a sense of purpose, and remain driven despite setbacks and obstacles. Highly motivated individuals and leaders have a strong internal drive and are able to tap into their intrinsic motivation. They can maintain a positive mindset, bounce back from setbacks, and maintain focus.

How to assess your level of emotional intelligence as a leader

Assessing your own level of emotional intelligence as a corporate leader is the first step to improving your skills in this critical area. Leaders who have high emotional intelligence have better relations with employees, make better decisions, and create a more productive work environment.

One way to assess your level of emotional intelligence is to begin by **evaluating your current self-awareness**. (Some companies call this **self-assessment**.) First, analyze your leadership style, looking for any negative behavior or language patterns that cause conflict or diminish team morale. Next, rank your strengths and see how they compare with your competencies in communication, emotional regulation, empathy, and social skills. You can also use **360-degree evaluations** to gain input from colleagues, supervisors, and direct reports. Whether by examining your self-care behaviors, listening capacity, and mentorship skills or mitigating emotional distress in others, these critical approaches to emotional intelligence modes can strengthen overall results.

You might also reflect on the values and principles you sincerely hold. *Harvard Business Review's* 10 Must Reads on High Performance advises doing a **mirror test** whereby you reflect on your actions and choices to determine if they align with your core values.

You could reflect on many values and leadership styles and underline what you think resembles you. Include it in your 360-degree feedback and see how many matches you get!

Values

Integrity – Honesty – Respect – Responsibility – Loyalty – Perseverance – Compassion – Empathy – Fairness – Trustworthiness – Courage – Humility – Open-mindedness – Authenticity – Accountability – Generosity – Kindness – Self-discipline – Gratitude – Independence – Optimism – Patience – Resilience – Creativity – Teamwork – Harmony – Balance – Adaptability – Ambition – Excellence – Curiosity – Innovation – Flexibility – Reliability – Determination – Selflessness – Tolerance – Self-improvement – Learning – Simplicity – Equality – Environmental sustainability – Spirituality – Wellness – Freedom – Adventure – Stability – Justice – Patriotism – Family

Leadership styles

Autocratic – Democratic – Laissez-faire – Transformational – Transactional – Servant – Charismatic – Adaptive – Bureaucratic – Authentic – Collaborative – Visionary – Participative – Coaching – Results-driven – Supportive – Analytical – Inspirational – Directing – Consensus-building – Relationship-oriented – Task-oriented – Cross-cultural – Relational – Strategic – Hands-on – Change-oriented – Results-oriented – Trust-building – Diplomatic – Facilitative – Resilient – Project-based – Empowering – Goal-oriented – Trustworthy

Additionally, individuals can take an **online emotional intelligence personality assessment**. Scoring well in fluidity between these competencies reflects flourishing leadership skills. These tests can provide insight into your own strengths and weaknesses and allow you to determine areas in which you need to improve. They may reveal which subcomponents you exhibit in low or high quantities. There are many popular online assessments, such as the Myers–Briggs Type Indicator, StrengthsFinder, and the Emotional Quotient Assessment. But remember, online assessments might be inaccurate, so use them as a secondary tool.

Evaluate your self-awareness by creating a realistic metric with the help of 360-degree feedback, comparison scoring using an EI test, skilled communication, empathy assessment, positive interpersonal skills, and healthy conflict-resolution tactics. These are the best ways to strengthen your emotional intelligence as a corporate leader.

The benefits of greater emotional intelligence, both for you and your team

For themselves, emotionally intelligent leaders often experience higher levels of productivity and resilience. Numerous research studies have demonstrated that emotionally intelligent leaders foster individuals dynamically in problem-solving, strategic planning, and sustaining productive and meaningful employee engagement. Improving one's emotional intelligence often paves the way to higher self-confidence and rapport with others, leading to network scalability and the achievement of personal and professional goals.

For the team, an emotionally intelligent leader provides colleagues with an inspirational and fulfilling journey based on proficiency, vision, and transparency. Leaders with high emotional intelligence can identify and mitigate disputes and establish strengthened team-building capacities. Consequently, they drive smoother workflow patterns by devising efficient data-driven problem-solving strategies that match changing business philosophies. Leaders move proactively, executing a blend of aptitude and innovation, which leads to a unique teamwork spirit.

Strategies for developing greater levels of emotional intelligence as a leader

Developing greater emotional intelligence as a corporate leader is an ongoing process that requires continuous learning, growth, and self-reflection. Don't think of it as a one-time exercise in your career. Think of it as annual maintenance. Here are some strategies for developing greater emotional intelligence as a corporate leader:

1. **Practice self-reflection** and **self-awareness**: Start by understanding your own thoughts and emotions and how they affect your actions, decisions, and communication with others. Recognize your emotional triggers, strengths, and limitations, and work on managing them effectively. Developing heightened self-awareness helps you work on blind spots that compromise effective decision-making and adaptive leadership styles.
2. **Develop empathy**: Focus on developing empathy toward colleagues and support judgment-free partnerships by showcasing the impact of EQ skills in the work environment. Learn to put yourself in other people's shoes, listen actively, and understand their perspectives. Developing empathy will not only help you as a leader, but it will also improve your customers' personal and professional relationships.
3. **Engage in active listening**: Effective and close-knit problem-solving and communication is vital in corporate leadership. Understand how your peers feel and consider their suggestions as well as feedback. Active listening is where you understand the message the other individual is conveying and respond coherently, leading to productive outcomes. One of the things I notice people doing is looking at their phone or laptop screen while talking to someone else. Or even worse, when you are on a conference call without turning on the camera, and the person you are talking to is doing something else. Practice being present when you are talking to your team. Try not to look at your phone. Even

holding your phone while talking to someone may distract you from the conversation.
4. **Attend EQ training programs**: Attending corporate leadership training programs provides an avenue for exchanging ideas concerning what works. Programs also include guest speakers and experts providing modern EQ strategic methods and problem-solving tactics necessary for both team and organization handling. Training can be helpful. However, just like reading this book, if you do not practice and move toward your goal, the training will not be very helpful.
5. **Collaborate with mentors and coaches**: Expanding insights toward mentors can result in successful emotional growth while promoting self-reflection principles and individual development channels, deepening the competencies essential in leading multi-faceted workplace needs.

How to leverage empathy to better understand and motivate team members

Empathy is a vital component of emotional intelligence. Leaders who possess it know how to leverage their emotional sensitivity towards their team members to better understand and motivate them. Being empathetic means deeply understanding and sharing the feelings of those around you. Empathetic leaders encourage greater awareness of feelings and actions within their workplace, allowing for exceptional awareness of their team's diverse and direct needs and pushing toward more coordinated, positive team-driven associations.

Here are three ways leaders can leverage empathy to better understand and motivate team members:

1. **Start by building trust:** A trusting relationship is at the core of any empathetic leadership style. Present yourself in such a way that motivates individuals and colleagues to build an equitable environment conducive to dynamic skill-building capabilities, followed by productive outcome motivations that enhance productivity and goodwill among team members. When practicing empathy, pay particular attention to self-regulation, which will help build trust within employee networks.
2. **Listen with intent:** Empathic leaders listen actively and present well-versed aural comprehension across team members. The environment created by effective listening with conciliatory intent initiates a more harmonious and trusting discourse, hence less friction. Emotional balance, shared pride, and camaraderie toward one another are positive outcomes of elevated empathy.
3. **Encourage open communication:** Followers encouraged to exchange ideas and opinions and give feedback increase their emotional responsiveness toward individual preferences, staying effective in addressing the motivations

and behavioral patterns necessary for teamwork synergistic evolution. Leadership that encourages open communication chambers supports positive expressions that build future-oriented patterns. These patterns generate creative, dynamic approaches to problem-solving.

2

LEADING WITH AUTHENTICITY

"Authentic leadership requires self-reflection and self-awareness, as it is through understanding oneself that true leadership emerges."

— PETER DRUCKER

Corporate leadership can be an elusive art. It requires finesse, vision, and a deep understanding of the human psyche. We have all heard of hundreds of leadership theories and styles—it seems there is no right or wrong. But I have noticed that the worst leadership style is when you pretend and try to be something you are not.

At the heart of good leadership is authenticity in all its forms. Authenticity has become a buzzword in the corporate world, but for good reason. As a concept, it speaks to what it means to be a leader in the modern world. Authenticity challenges leaders to take a hard look at themselves, their motivations, and their values. How often do you think leaders do that amid daily corporate demands? But when they do, they unlock the ability to build connections and inspire and motivate their teams in powerful ways.

So, what does authentic leadership really mean? It means being yourself and acting in ways that are consistent with your personal values. To be authentic, leaders should be self-aware and emotionally intelligent, which we discussed earlier in the book. They should understand the motivations of others and be able to empathize with their struggles. Authentic leaders validate their team members, encouraging them to voice their opinions and take risks.

While authenticity is a critical ingredient for success as a leader, it is not always easy to achieve. It takes practice, reflection, and a willingness to learn and grow. Leaders who embrace authenticity, however, will find that it is the key to unlocking their potential and creating a corporate culture that inspires and motivates their teams to achieve great things.

Benefits of authentic leadership—both for leaders and their teams

So, what are the benefits of authentic leadership in the corporate world, and why should you care?

The first benefit is **trust**. Authentic leaders are known for their transparency, openness, and honesty. They are not afraid to show their vulnerabilities and mistakes, and they share their goals and vision for the company clearly and honestly. This type of leadership trusts team members, making it easier for leaders to build and maintain meaningful relationships both within and outside the organization. The problem with cherry-picking behaviors from different leadership styles, or behaving in a way that is not in line with your values, is consistency. Your team is watching you more than you know—every move, every gesture, and every comment you make. Once they see that your behaviors do not add up and lack consistency and authenticity, it will be very difficult for them to trust you. And if you want to position yourself as a leader, trust is the first thing you need to win in your team.

> *"No matter your title, people will not follow you if they don't trust you. Whether you are just taking over a team or working to implement large-scale change within one, you are guaranteed to run into resistance if you haven't taken time to establish a foundation with the people you oversee before turning their worlds upside down."*
>
> — JOHN C. MAXWELL
> AUTHOR & FOUNDER OF THE JOHN MAXWELL
> LEADERSHIP FOUNDATION

The second benefit is **engagement**. Authentic leaders who are transparent about their values and beliefs create an engaging and inclusive workplace culture that inspires the team to work toward a shared vision. Authentic leaders value and promote innovation, creativity, and collaboration. They are in the unique position to foster a positive and inclusive work environment that helps everyone feel a sense of belonging and purpose—which, in turn, leads to higher levels of engagement and productivity. A highly engaged team is hard to beat, which is why one of the metrics most multinational companies assess when they measure leadership effectiveness is employee engagement. It is also an indicator of the sustainability of the team and the organization.

The third benefit is **adaptability**. Authentic leaders are often more adaptable than their less authentic counterparts. They are flexible in their approach, willing to learn new ways of doing things, and able to respond to changing market conditions and stakeholder needs. This level of adaptability is critical in today's fast-paced and ever-changing corporate world. I am sure most of us have worked with autocratic leaders—the type of leader who has one way of doing things no matter the circumstances, and finds it almost impossible to admit they are ever wrong. In today's climate, those leaders will not survive.

The fourth benefit is **strength**: the strength that comes with diversity and inclusion. Authentic leaders appreciate and embrace diversity in all its forms. They create an inclusive culture where everyone's voice is respected, leading to innovation, creativity, and diverse perspectives. These diverse perspectives drive organizational success in an increasingly diverse world. Later, I will speak more about how to lead teams that value diversity and how essential diversity and inclusion are to your success. I will also acknowledge the challenges they present and share ideas for overcoming these challenges.

Supporting all of the above, authentic leaders base their decisions on their core values, principles, and moral compass—their **true north**. This consistency provides a solid foundation for decision-making, guiding leaders to make choices aligned with the organization's vision and long-term success.

Authentic leadership sets the tone for an entire organization. When leaders prioritize authenticity, it permeates the whole company, creating a **positive and empowering culture** that attracts top talent, enhances employee satisfaction, and fosters a sense of belonging and purpose among employees.

Nature or nurture?

Although authentic leadership is often considered an innate trait, research has found that these skills can be developed and honed over time. Developing authentic leadership skills can be a challenging but deeply rewarding process.

Below are listed several strategies that aspiring leaders can use to help cultivate their own authenticity and strengthen their unique leadership style.

The first strategy is to **focus on self-reflection** because it will help you with every aspect of your life, including understanding your inner motives, values, and purpose. Authentic leaders are self-aware and are intentional about their actions and behaviors. To cultivate these skills, leaders should make time to reflect on their core values, strengths, and weaknesses. They may wish to seek feedback from colleagues. When was the last time you asked for 360-degree feedback? And I don't mean simply asking the people you get along with in the office. You can also attend leadership development programs that encourage self-awareness. Through this self-reflection, leaders gain a deeper understanding of themselves and their leadership style. Dedicate some time every day or every week to self-reflection, and you will have more clarity about why you do what you do.

The second strategy is to **build relationships based on trust and honesty**. Authentic leaders prioritize building meaningful relationships with team members, customers, and stakeholders. Leaders can cultivate this skill by actively listening to others, providing feedback that is both honest and constructive, and being open to diverse perspectives and ideas.

The third strategy is to **promote a culture of authenticity**. We will discuss culture in more depth as it is one of the most important roles of a leader. Leaders can facilitate an environment where team members feel safe and supported to express their authentic selves. This might mean rewarding vulnerability and courage, openly discussing mistakes and failures, and embracing diversity and inclusiveness. Authentic leaders prioritize creating a positive and inclusive workplace culture where everyone feels valued, respected, and heard.

The fourth is to **develop oneself as a leader**. Authentic leadership is a journey that requires continuous growth and development. Leaders can continue to develop their skills through coaching, mentorship, and accepting learning opportunities. They might attend conferences or workshops, read leadership literature, or seek job experiences that challenge them to learn new skills or build on their strengths.

Overcoming the biggest barrier to authentic leadership: fear of showing vulnerability

While authentic leadership is essential in the corporate world, it can be hard to practice. Leaders may encounter barriers that prevent them from fully embracing their authenticity. Showing one's vulnerability, in particular, can be perceived as a weakness in organizational cultures where leaders are expected to always appear strong, assertive, and invulnerable. Many such leaders confuse being obnoxious, self-centered, or autocratic with strength and confidence—in fact, they are the opposite of confidence.

Fortunately, if you work in such a culture, there are practical strategies that you can use to overcome this and other barriers and develop your authenticity. And being an authentic leader will give you an edge.

The first strategy is to **embrace discomfort and uncertainty**. Authentic leadership requires courage and a willingness to take risks. Leaders need to recognize that making themselves vulnerable can have benefits. By acknowledging their weaknesses and imperfections, they create an environment where others do the same, and the leaders can then guide the team to growth and development. Leaders can practice embracing vulnerability by taking incremental steps, seeking feedback from others, and reframing failures as learning opportunities.

The second strategy is to **seek and build a support system**. Leaders need support and guidance as they navigate the challenges of leadership. They should identify those individuals who support and encourage them to build their strength and resilience. Whether you are leading a business or a support function, you need to have a support team and, ideally, be part of someone else's support team. Being involved in supporting others will help you in your everyday job. Leadership coaching, mentorship, or support groups are great ways of connecting with other leaders and having positive conversations, building the right problem-solving skills and ideas to help combat the fear of vulnerability.

The third strategy is to **embrace a growth mindset** and **practice continuous learning**. Authentic leaders acknowledge they don't know everything and are always open to new ideas and perspectives. When fear of vulnerability kicks in, remember there is always room to grow. Personal and professional development can help leaders improve their strengths and overcome their weaknesses. If you stop learning because you have a history of success, this might be the end of your success. You do not want to be that leader who became outdated with the technology and innovation because you thought you knew enough.

Finally, authenticity in leadership comes from **integrating business goals with personal values and vision**, creating a cohesive guiding light for the team's and stakeholders' contributions. Authenticity is also achieved when the leader refrains from making decisions solely based on business objectives and is driven to do what's right over what is easy or profitable. This could be one of the hardest things to balance—but once you find that balance, decision-making will become very easy.

The fear of vulnerability is a common barrier to authentic leadership. However, with the right strategy and commitment, leaders can overcome this fear and embrace self-discovery, thus creating better environments for their teams to grow and prosper.

Examples of authentic leaders and what sets them apart

One example of an authentic leader is **Oprah Winfrey**. Oprah has been vocal about her challenging childhood, including her experiences of poverty, discrimination, and abuse. These experiences have shaped her leadership style, making her more empathetic and relatable to others. Through her many roles in the media industry, Oprah has used her platform to inspire people to be their best selves, to create more significant change in their communities, and to live authentically.

A second example is **Satya Nadella**, the CEO of Microsoft. Since assuming his role in 2014, Satya has prioritized inclusivity, empathy, and innovation. One of his most significant contributions to the company's culture has been to create an openness to new ideas and experimentation. In demonstrating his commitment to these values, Satya has overseen a revamped company culture, leading to greater employee engagement and business success.

A third example is **Howard Schultz**, the former CEO of Starbucks. Schultz has been vocal about his difficult childhood and the challenges he faced when starting his career. One of the hallmarks of his leadership is his commitment to corporate social responsibility. He has been committed to making a difference wherever Starbucks operates, taking stands on various social issues, and prioritizing employee benefits and well-being.

The final example I am presenting is **Bob Iger** (former CEO of Walt Disney Company). Iger's authenticity stands out through his ability to foster creativity, innovation, and storytelling. Iger transformed Disney into a global entertainment powerhouse by emphasizing quality content and memorable experiences. His approachable manner and deep appreciation for the company's heritage have made him an admired leader inside and outside Disney.

These examples illustrate the key traits of authentic leaders. Authenticity, empathy, and the willingness to take risks are fundamental elements of their leadership styles. By being true to themselves and leading by example, they inspire their teams and colleagues to achieve great things. Whether in the media, tech, or consumer goods industries, these individuals show that authentic leadership is possible and can make a considerable difference in the corporate world and beyond.

3

THE INNER BATTLE—OVERCOMING SELF-DOUBT AND IMPOSTER SYNDROME

Understanding self-doubt—its causes and what you can do about it—is crucial for developing leadership potential. Self-doubt, often resulting from a lack of confidence in one's abilities or a fear of failure, is a common obstacle many aspiring leaders face. A prevalent cause of self-doubt, wherein individuals doubt their own accomplishments and fear exposure as frauds, is "imposter syndrome". It can hinder the development of leadership skills and cause individuals to question their worth and potential. By recognizing and addressing self-doubt, leaders can cultivate the confidence to unlock their full potential and lead with conviction.

Researchers have identified self-doubt as a significant barrier to leadership development. A study by Howard et al. (2019) found that self-doubt negatively impacts leadership self-efficacy, which influences one's belief in one's capability to lead effectively. Furthermore, a study by Koenig et al. (2011) has highlighted the detrimental impact of self-doubt on decision-making processes and the ability to take risks as a leader. These findings emphasize the importance of acknowledging self-doubt as a valid challenge that leaders must overcome to develop their leadership potential.

By embracing self-doubt as a natural part of the leadership journey, you can take steps to build your confidence and confront your insecurities. Engaging in self-reflection, seeking feedback from mentors or coaches, and focusing on personal growth can help leaders address their self-doubt. Developing a growth mindset, setting realistic goals, and celebrating small wins along the way can also boost confidence and counteract self-doubt. Ultimately, understanding and overcoming self-doubt is a transformative process that empowers leaders to embrace their true potential and excel in their roles.

Identifying the psychological causes and effects of self-doubt

Self-doubt is a complex psychological phenomenon that can arise from various causes and damage individuals' personal and professional lives. Here are some causes and effects of self-doubt:

1. **Fear of failure:** When individuals worry about not meeting their own or others' expectations, they may doubt their ability to succeed.
2. **Society's standards:** Societal pressures to conform and meet certain standards can contribute to self-doubt. Unrealistic media portrayals and societal norms shape expectations, making individuals compare themselves to others and question their worth.
3. **Perfectionism:** Individuals striving for perfection often battle self-doubt, fearing they will never measure up to their own impossibly high standards. Perfectionism creates a constant feeling of scrutiny, stalling progress and fueling self-doubt.
4. **Imposter syndrome:** Imposter syndrome is a prevalent cause of self-doubt, wherein individuals doubt their own accomplishments and fear exposure as frauds. Despite evidence of their competence, they persistently feel unworthy and doubt their abilities.
5. **Negative experiences**: Negative experiences such as criticism or the memory of failure can linger and contribute to self-doubt. Past setbacks can lead individuals to question their abilities, affecting their self-confidence and perpetuating self-doubt.
6. **Lack of a supportive environment**: When individuals lack a supportive environment that provides encouragement, feedback, and recognition, their belief in themselves can waver. Without support from others, self-doubt may intensify, hindering growth and achievement.
7. **Overwhelming challenges and uncertainty**: When faced with tough situations or uncertainties, individuals may

doubt their ability to handle them. Fear of the unknown can trigger self-doubt, erode confidence, and inhibit progress.
8. **Negative self-talk:** Negative self-talk, characterized by self-criticism and self-demeaning language, can contribute to self-doubt. Constant negative reinforcement internally convinces individuals of their limitations.

The impacts of self-doubt can be far-reaching, stifling personal and professional growth, hampering decision-making, and inhibiting individuals from seizing opportunities. Self-doubt can manifest as avoidance of challenges, missed career advancements, strained relationships, and diminished self-worth. Additionally, self-doubt can decrease motivation and performance as individuals hesitate to take risks or pursue their goals.

To combat self-doubt, individuals should address its causes head-on. Encouraging a positive mindset, seeking support and feedback, fostering self-compassion, and challenging negative thought patterns can alleviate self-doubt. Cultivating self-confidence, embracing failure as a learning opportunity, and celebrating strengths and accomplishments are essential to overcoming self-doubt.

Developing techniques for managing self-doubt

Now that we know that managing self-doubt is crucial for leaders to unlock their full potential and lead with confidence, here

THE INNER BATTLE—OVERCOMING SELF-DOUBT

is a summary of the techniques you can employ to manage self-doubt when it arises:

1. **Embrace vulnerability**: Recognize that self-doubt is a human experience shared by us all, including leaders. Embracing vulnerability allows leaders to acknowledge their insecurities, seek support, and learn from their challenges, fostering personal growth.
2. **Practice self-reflection**: Engage in regular self-reflection to gain self-awareness and understand the underlying causes of self-doubt. Identify patterns, triggers, and self-limiting beliefs. This introspective practice enables leaders to develop strategies for managing and overcoming self-doubt.
3. **Build a support network**: Surround yourself with a network of mentors, coaches, or trusted colleagues who can provide guidance, perspective, and encouragement. Seeking advice and leaning on others can help combat self-doubt and provide reassurance.
4. **Cultivate self-compassion**: Treat yourself with kindness and self-compassion. Practice positive self-talk, celebrate accomplishments, and remind yourself of your strengths and past successes.
5. **Set realistic goals:** Break down big goals into achievable milestones. Setting realistic and attainable goals helps build confidence and allows for steady progress. If you celebrate each milestone reached, this will reinforce a positive mindset.
6. **Focus on your strengths**: Identify and leverage your unique strengths as a leader. Recognize the value and

expertise you bring to the table. By focusing on your strengths, you can enhance your self-confidence and mitigate self-doubt.

7. **Seek feedback**: Actively seek feedback from trusted sources to gain insights into your strengths and areas for improvement. Constructive feedback can help dispel self-doubt and provide guidance for professional development.
8. **Practice resilience**: Cultivate resilience by reframing setbacks as learning opportunities. Embrace failure as a valuable part of the leadership journey, focusing on continuous improvement rather than dwelling on self-doubt.
9. **Cultivate a growth mindset**: A growth mindset embraces challenges and views failure as an opportunity for growth. Fostering a belief in your potential to learn and improve will help you combat self-doubt and encourage personal development.

By implementing these techniques, leaders can proactively manage self-doubt, cultivate confidence, and excel in their roles.

Identifying and avoiding the comparison trap

In today's interconnected world, social media and other platforms often lure people into the comparison trap by showcasing only the highlights and carefully curated portions of others' lives. They make it all too easy to fall into the trap of comparing oneself to others, whether peers, industry leaders, or even social media influencers. However, such comparisons are often based on incomplete information and can lead to a skewed perception of one's own abilities and accomplishments.

As we scroll through our feeds, we are bombarded with images of successful, happy, and seemingly flawless lives, which can lead us to believe that others are thriving while we are falling behind. This portrayal represents only a fraction of reality, and by fixating on this limited version, we fail to see the full picture. Behind the polished façade lie private struggles, failures, and insecurities. It is essential to remember that what we see on social media is a heavily filtered version of others' lives, and comparing ourselves solely based on that can lead to feelings of inadequacy and undermine our own well-being.

It is paramount for a leader to identify and avoid the comparison trap, because it can perpetuate self-doubt and hinder personal and professional growth.

The research supports the danger of comparisons. Friesen et al. (2020) suggest that comparing oneself to others can negatively affect mental well-being and self-esteem. This can create a vicious cycle of self-doubt, as leaders may constantly feel inadequate compared to their perceived competition. Furthermore, a study by Mussweiler and Regner (2013) found that individuals tend to compare themselves selectively to those who outperform them, leading to further feelings of self-doubt.

To avoid the comparison trap, leaders should focus on self-awareness and self-acceptance. Recognize that everyone's journey is unique, and that success and progress are subjective. Embrace a mindset of growth and continuous improvement, where the goal is to become the best version of yourself rather than attempting to match the achievements of others.

Leaders should also cultivate gratitude and celebrate their own accomplishments. Recognize the progress made and the positive impact created by your own leadership. Surround yourself with a supportive network that recognizes and appreciates your unique strengths. It will help reinforce self-confidence and mitigate self-doubt.

By remaining focused on personal growth, self-acceptance, and acknowledging individual achievements, leaders can navigate the comparison trap and develop self-assuredness and authenticity in their leadership journey.

4

BECOMING BULLETPROOF

In today's fast-paced and increasingly demanding corporate landscape, we often find ourselves consumed by the pursuit of success, leaving little room to prioritize our health and well-being. However, we should recognize that for sustained performance and for leading teams to new heights, taking care of our physical and mental health is essential.

I've had the privilege of interviewing many CEOs, presidents, and senior leaders around the world across industries who have shared valuable insights on the role of well-being in their personal and professional lives. Most of them wished they had made it a priority earlier in their career. Many shared the "bio hacks" that worked for them in their extremely busy lives.

Your health is your most valuable asset, a foundational pillar that supports your longevity and long-term effectiveness as a leader. Neglecting it today may bring problems in the future. Therefore, it is crucial to redirect your attention to your well-being and invest in sustainable practices that will enable you to thrive.

Thankfully, there are numerous quick wins and simple bio hacks to help you dramatically improve your well-being. This chapter will delve deeper into these exciting bio hacks and practical methods for enhancing well-being. Remember, pick whatever you feel fits your lifestyle, and I would always suggest consulting a reliable coach to support you on the journey.

Breathe

Breathing is intuitive. We have all been doing it from birth. However, due to human devolution in the past couple of hundred years, we have been sitting more than ever, which has impacted our posture. When we sit for long periods, our bodies adapt by hunching forward, which compresses our chest cavity and restricts our ability to take deep breaths. Additionally, our modern lifestyle has led us to consume more processed and industrial food, which has had a detrimental effect on our facial and jaw structure. These changes have caused our air pathways to become smaller, making it harder for us to breathe freely.

James Nestor, the author of *Breath*, extensively researched the impact of our modern lifestyle on breathing. He found that these changes in our posture and diet have led to a number of respiratory issues, including chronic mouth breathing. This is a problem because nasal breathing is essential for activating the parasympathetic nervous system, responsible for rest and recovery. On the other hand, mouth breathing can activate the sympathetic nervous system, which puts our bodies in a constant state of stress and survival mode.

Additionally, Nestor discovered that nasal breathing increases the production of nitric oxide sixfold. Nitric oxide has numerous health benefits, such as improving blood flow, regulating blood pressure, enhancing immune function, and promoting better sleep. By breathing through our noses, we can harness these benefits and support our overall well-being.

If we want to optimize our cognitive abilities, health, and focus, we must also consider the carbon dioxide levels in our environment. Poor ventilation can lead to an increase in carbon dioxide levels, which can have a significant impact on our cognitive functions. Studies have shown that elevated carbon dioxide levels in places such as bars and aircraft can reach up to 4,000 parts per million. In such environments, our cognitive abilities can be compromised, leading to decreased productivity and performance.

It is important to note that even lower levels of carbon dioxide can have an impact. For example, a two-year collaborative study by the Massachusetts Institute of Technology, Maastricht University (the Netherlands), and University College London showed that when carbon dioxide levels reached 800 parts per million, students experienced a 20% decrease in test results. In contrast, outdoor carbon dioxide levels typically hover around 400 parts per million, which is considered healthy. Therefore, if you are working on an important project or need to maintain focus, it is crucial to ensure you are in a well-ventilated space with fresh air circulation.

Additionally, studies have shown that longevity and lifespan are directly linked to lung capacity. By improving our breathing techniques and lung capacity, we can enhance our overall health and potentially extend our lifespan. One effective way to improve lung capacity is to focus on diaphragmatic breathing, which involves engaging the diaphragm muscle while breathing deeply. This technique allows for increased oxygen intake and better lung expansion.

Poor breathing habits can contribute to a range of health issues, including autoimmune diseases, inflammation, anxiety, and various other ailments. When we breathe improperly, we disrupt the balance of oxygen and carbon dioxide in our bodies, leading to physiological imbalances and increased stress on our systems.

In conclusion, improving our breathing habits is key to enhancing our resilience and well-being. To support this goal, here are some practical tips.

1. Practice diaphragmatic breathing. Put your hands over your hip bones and breathe laterally.
2. Use a breathing pattern of five to six seconds for inhalation and exhalation to promote relaxation and balance.

3. Maintain good posture to allow for optimal breathing.
4. Incorporate regular exercise, specifically activities that promote cardiovascular fitness, to strengthen respiratory muscles and improve lung capacity by about 20%.
5. Create a well-ventilated environment with fresh air circulation to ensure optimal carbon dioxide levels and cognitive function.
6. Avoid chronic mouth breathing and prioritize nasal breathing throughout the day.
7. Consider practicing mindfulness or meditation techniques that emphasize breath awareness to promote relaxation and reduce stress.
8. Seek out resources and education on proper breathing techniques, such as books like *Breath* by James Nestor or online courses.
9. Take breaks throughout the day to focus on deep breathing and relaxation exercises.

By incorporating these tips into our daily lives and understanding the importance of proper breathing, we can empower ourselves to optimize our resilience, well-being, and cognitive performance.

Meditate and practice non-sleep deep rest (NSDR)

Do not skip this part even if you are skeptical about meditation. Athletes, entrepreneurs, and many successful individuals practice meditation daily for a reason. Over the past few decades, extensive research has been conducted on meditation and mindfulness, with brain monitoring through MRI or functional MRI providing insights into brain activity during meditation. Not only have these studies looked at brain changes during meditation, but they have also evaluated emotional and performance outcomes afterward.

What happens to your brain when you meditate? By closing your eyes, sitting in a comfortable position, removing distractions, and focusing on your breath, you can experience the slowing of brain waves from beta to alpha, delta, and theta frequencies. Our brain operates at different frequencies depending on our state of consciousness. Beta waves (14–40 Hz) are associated with wakefulness and alertness. Alpha waves (8–13 Hz) occur when we are in a relaxed and calm state, with an inward focus. Delta waves (0.5–4 Hz), the slowest brainwaves, are experienced during dreamless sleep or deep states of unconsciousness. Theta waves (4–8 Hz) are linked to deep relaxation, creativity, and meditation.

The process of slowing brain waves to these lower frequencies typically involves focused breathing and concentration. Practice deep, slow-breathing techniques to induce a calm state of mind and engage the relaxation response. In this state, the brain transitions from beta to alpha, then further into theta and delta frequencies. Tools such as guided meditations, binaural beats, or mindfulness techniques can also assist in achieving these slower brainwave patterns.

Reaching alpha, delta, and theta wave states during meditation offers numerous benefits. First and foremost, these states facilitate deep relaxation and stress reduction, providing a sense of rejuvenation and restfulness. Slowing brainwaves also cultivate greater self-awareness, intuition, and inner peace. Alpha and theta waves are especially associated with enhanced creativity and profound insights. The mind becomes more open to new ideas and perspectives, fostering a heightened level of inspiration during meditation.

Different meditation books or individuals may suggest varying techniques, but for the sake of simplicity, here is a basic approach:

1. Try to meditate in the morning when your brain is already in an alpha state.
2. Find a comfortable environment and remove distractions.
3. Lie down in a comfortable position.
4. Bring your attention to your breath, naturally breathing in through your nose and out through your mouth.
5. Focus your awareness on different parts of your body and consciously release muscular tension.
6. Choose a point of focus, such as your breath, a mantra, visualization, or an object of concentration, and direct your attention toward it.

7. When your mind wanders, acknowledge thoughts without judgment or attachment, then guide your attention back.
8. Count backward from 50 or 100 slowly—to help in the beginning, imagine drawing each number as you count.

Once you're completely relaxed, you can engage in various activities:

- Visualize successful moments in your life.
- Visualize loved ones and feel the emotions of love, care, and trust.
- Visualize a detailed future you desire, including a job, house, or relationship.
- Repeat positive affirmations or mantras, such as "I am calm and peaceful" or "I am surrounded by abundance."
- Explore different visualization techniques.
- Bring your attention back to your body and surroundings before opening your eyes.
- Start wiggling your fingers and toes, stretch gently, and gradually open your eyes.

Remember, the duration of your meditation can be as short as five minutes or as long as you wish. The longer you meditate, the more mystical it becomes.

Prioritize a good night's sleep

I deeply admire those who prioritize and value their sleep. Unfortunately, some people believe they can function optimally with minimal sleep, even considering it a sign of strength to stay awake for long hours. Others see themselves as exceptions, believing their bodies require fewer hours of sleep than most people. However, according to Arianna Huffington, author of *The Sleep Revolution*, only about 1% of people can be classified as short sleepers who can function well with less than eight hours of sleep. Short sleep is not a skill that can be learned.

As stated by Dr. Judith Owens, Director of the Center for Pediatric Sleep Disorders at Boston's Children's Hospital, getting enough sleep is just as crucial as good nutrition, physical activity, or wearing a seatbelt. Sleep researcher Allan Rechtschaffen from the University of Chicago points out that if sleep did not serve a vital function, it would be the biggest mistake in the evolutionary process. Moreover, lack of sleep can have effects equivalent to alcohol consumption and may lead to diseases such as diabetes, heart problems, high blood pressure, and strokes. Additionally, it can cause accidents, memory problems, unhealthy eating habits, depression, skin issues, and other negative effects on individuals and those around them.

While it's true that some people identify as either owls or larks due to their natural sleep preferences, most of us fall in the middle. Daniel Pink refers to this group as "third birds" in his book, *When: The Scientific Secrets of Perfect Timing*. To determine your chronotype, consider your sleeping habits during your time off when you don't have any exceptional circumstances, such as staying out until the early hours of the morning. Calculate the midpoint between your bedtime and waking time. If it falls between 3:00 a.m. and 5:00 a.m., you are neither an owl nor a lark—you fall in the middle of the pack.

Sleep was a constant struggle for me until the end of last year. It left me frustrated and helpless, spending nights tossing and turning and desperately longing for the effortless sleep others seemed to enjoy. I recognized the need for guidance and a deeper understanding of sleep, which led me to consult a sleep therapist and extensively research the topic. During my research, I came across an invaluable resource: Matthew Walker, the esteemed author of *Why We Sleep*. Walker's profound insights shed light on the mysteries of sleep and provided information that resonated with my experience.

If you are one of the fortunate who can effortlessly slip into a blissful sleep every night, consider yourself blessed. However, if you, like the majority of us, struggle with the elusive nature of sleep, I have gathered several tips inspired by Matthew Walker that are bound to improve the quality of your sleep:

1. Maintain a regular sleep schedule by going to bed and waking up at the same time every day. This helps regulate your internal body clock.

2. Get sun exposure on your skin and spend time outdoors during sunset to help regulate your circadian rhythm.
3. Create a dark sleeping environment by switching off overhead lights an hour before bed.
4. Sleep in a cool bedroom with a temperature of around 18.5 degrees Celsius for optimal sleep.
5. Follow the 30-minute rule—if you can't fall asleep within 30 minutes, get out of bed. Go for a walk or practice meditation.
6. Limit alcohol consumption as it reduces the quality of sleep.
7. Reduce exposure to blue light from screens at night, even when using night mode on your devices.
8. If you need to use your phone in the bedroom, use it while standing up to minimize engagement and exposure to blue light.
9. Avoid daytime napping or limit it to 20 minutes to prevent sleep inertia.
10. Avoid caffeinated drinks close to bedtime. Caffeine negatively affects sleep quality, with a half-life of five to six hours and a quarter-life of ten to twelve hours.
11. Let go of worry and avoid pressuring yourself to fall asleep.
12. Read something before attempting to go to sleep. Reading helps many people fall asleep, but it may not work for everyone.
13. Remove clocks from the bedroom to prevent clock-watching.
14. Practice a few minutes of meditation before bed to relax your mind and body.
15. Wear glasses that block blue light after sunset or a couple of hours before bedtime.

16. Consider taking 500 to 600 mg of magnesium each night to help relax your body.
17. Engage in regular exercise but not close to bedtime.
18. Accept that a good night's sleep is not always guaranteed. Letting go of the pressure to sleep can sometimes help you drift off more easily.

Prioritize hydration

You may be wondering why I've dedicated a section to hydration, as it should be common knowledge. However, I'd like to present some current data in the hope that you'll prioritize hydration in the right way.

Being in a demanding job, especially in a leadership position, requires you to be in good physical and mental shape. Quick thinking, creativity, and prompt decision-making are essential at this level. To perform optimally, we cannot afford to have brain fog, headaches, or low energy. Many people turn to medication and painkillers to get through the day before considering the simplest, cheapest, and most readily available option: water. It is often assumed that we drink enough water, but research shows that in the USA alone, 75% of Americans are chronically dehydrated, consuming less than three cups a day. A study by Loughborough University in the UK revealed that a mere 2% of body weight loss due to dehydration can lead to impaired cognitive performance and reduced physical capabilities, including endurance and strength.

You probably already know that around 60% of your body is composed of water and that water is crucial to every aspect of life, from blood circulation to the proper functioning of organs. The list of side effects caused by dehydration is extensive, ranging from fatigue and weakness to dizziness and lightheadedness, headaches and migraines, poor skin health, impaired cognitive function, digestive issues, increased risk of heart-related illnesses, muscle cramps, rapid heartbeat, increased risk of kidney stones, decreased blood pressure, and many more. How can we expect to perform at our best with these potential side effects?

Dehydration can result from various factors, such as physical activity, inadequate fluid intake, certain diets, medications, and other influences. While drinking plain water is essential, it may not provide the necessary electrolytes and minerals needed to maintain the proper balance in our bodies. Here are some fundamental rules to help you stay hydrated:

1. Measure your fluid intake: Aim for 3.7 liters for men and 2.7 liters for women.
2. Add electrolytes to your water, such as sodium, potassium, and magnesium.
3. Sip water throughout the day instead of consuming large quantities all at once.
4. Set reminders if you tend to forget to drink water.

5. Infuse your water with ingredients like lemon, lime, cucumber, berries, etc., if you find plain water unappealing.
6. Consume water-rich foods: I enjoy having snacks like cucumbers at night.
7. Make it a habit to drink water before, during, and after every meal.
8. Hydrate before, during, and after exercising.
9. Pay attention to the color of your urine—the yellower it is, the more dehydrated you are.
10. Limit alcohol consumption.
11. Keep water within reach at all times.
12. Consider trying sparkling water if you enjoy the fizzy sensation.
13. For intense workouts, add salt and a bit of maple syrup to your water and drink it an hour before training.

By following these guidelines, you can prioritize hydration and ensure an adequate fluid intake throughout the day. Keep in mind that everyone's hydration needs may vary, so listen to your body's indicators and adjust accordingly.

Prioritize gut health and basic nutrition

We all desire to feel good and be happy all the time. But did you know that our happy chemicals and neurotransmitters are produced and stored in the gut? In fact, 95% of your total body serotonin and 50% of its dopamine are synthesized in your gut. Imbalances in the gut microbiome, which

is composed of trillions of bacteria, microbes, fungi, yeasts, and other organisms, can result in inflammation in the body. This inflammation can affect the brain and lead to anxiety, depression, and other health problems. By eating food that nourishes our bodies, we can improve our physical and mental well-being.

Nutrition is such a vast topic that I always recommend consulting a reliable nutritionist. As Kassandra Hobart (nutritionist and CrossFit Games athlete) emphasized in my interview with her, "Bio-individuality is so different; our metabolism is also very different. Research has shown that there is no single diet that fits every single person." With that in mind, I will provide you with a simple nutrition guide. Read it through to the end, as the final step is crucial and can improve every aspect of your life.

Let's begin by examining our current social lifestyle. When we meet up with friends, we often suggest going out for dinner, grabbing a bite, having a drink, meeting for coffee or brunch, or going out for lunch. Business meetings often involve lunches and dinners with colleagues. Many of our celebrations involve cakes, turkey, gravy, stuffing, sweets, and more. Even when we go to the movies, we have popcorn, nachos, M&Ms, and soft drinks. Our social lives revolve around food and beverages, and it's understandable because food can enhance the enjoyment of these experiences. However, it's important to note that we often eat for social events rather than according to what our bodies need. Kassandra Hobart highlighted a significant issue in our society—we have normalized unhealthy habits, and anyone who chooses to prioritize their health is often seen as peculiar or unconformable.

As a first step, I encourage you to **remain conscious** of everything you eat throughout the day without necessarily changing your current eating habits. Pay attention to every single item that enters your body. Be present when you eat, including snacks at your desk, sugar in your tea, chocolate bars, and any supplements you may be taking. If it's hard to remember everything, consider writing it down or using popular apps like MyFitnessPal, which allow you to log your food and even scan barcodes. Before going to bed or when you have a few minutes, review the list of everything you've consumed during the day and consider whether all of it was necessary. Were you truly hungry when you ate those biscuits, or did you have them simply because they were available? Reflect on the small items you ate and determine what, without much effort, you could do without. This is the easiest way to begin reducing excess calorie consumption. At this stage, we are primarily focusing on quantity rather than quality.

As a second step, **convert** your food intake into calories. This may be a new concept for some people, but it will help you understand your eating habits. Numerous applications, such as My Fitness Pal, Google, or even ChatGPT can assist you with this conversion. I recommend using an app as it will allow you to keep a history of your food consumption and offers additional functions. For instance, if you have a Big Tasty meal with fries and a Coke from McDonald's, you can find it listed on MyFitnessPal at around 1,400 calories. This will give you an idea of how many calories you consume per meal. Calories are units of energy obtained from food and beverages. Consequently, imagine you consume 4,000 calories a day and only burn 2,000 calories. Those extra 2,000 calories won't magically disappear! At this stage, we are still focusing on measuring calorie intake rather than the quality of food.

The third step is to **compare** your calorie intake to the calories you burn throughout the day. If you have a sedentary job, you can estimate an average of 2,000 calories for females and 2,500 calories for males per day. If you're more active and engage in regular exercise, your calorie needs may be slightly higher. In summary, there are three scenarios: if your goal is to lose weight, your calorie intake should be less than the calories you burn. If you want to maintain your weight, the intake and burned calories should be roughly equal. If you aim to gain weight, your intake should be higher than the calories burned. This simple approach allows you to track your calorie balance more effectively.

After gaining visibility on your daily calorie intake and assessing it in relation to your activity level, it becomes clear that some adjustments need to be made. This brings us to the fourth step: considering which calories to **cut**. If your eating habits are similar to mine, there are probably many areas where you can reduce calorie consumption. However, abruptly cutting a significant number of calories overnight may not be sustainable or beneficial for your body. Once you have identified your average daily calorie intake in step two, I suggest gradually reducing it by approximately 100 calories per week. Avoid making drastic changes to your calorie intake overnight; sustainability and a proper body response are key. For instance, if you typically add sugar to your coffee, have biscuits with your tea, and indulge in various unnecessary snacks, you can start by cutting back on some of these items or replacing them with healthier alternatives. I will address this further in the next step.

It is important to understand not only what you eat but how it affects your body. Simply maintaining a caloric balance might not necessarily provide the desired energy level and cognitive benefits. This is where the fifth step—**to clean** up your diet—becomes crucial. The definition of "healthy" varies from person to person. Some might believe that homemade food is healthy, while others may think that a diet consisting solely of greens is the best option. I won't prescribe a specific diet because it truly depends on the individual, but it is essential to gather basic information on nutrition regardless of your chosen diet.

Cleaning Tips:

- Opt for whole foods rather than processed foods.
- Diversify your food by consuming over 30 different types of food weekly.
- Prioritize protein in your meals.
- Reduce your intake of fried foods or switch to healthier oils like olive oil.
- Incorporate more greens and vegetables into your meals.

- Increase your fiber intake.
- Limit your sugar intake to manage insulin spikes.
- Cut out or reduce alcohol consumption.
- Bear in mind you don't need as much food as you might think.
- Stay hydrated.
- Reduce your consumption of packaged foods.

By following these steps, you keep track of your calorie intake and improve the quality of the food you consume. Keep in mind that when it comes to nutrition, it's a personal journey—what will suit one person may not suit another.

Recognize that sitting is the new smoking

One of the most significant health challenges in our modern society is the time we spend sitting. A negative effect of all that sitting is poor posture.

We humans are made to move, and it is more the lack of movement and variation that is the big killer, not a specific right or wrong position. If you stay in ANY position for too long, I promise you something will start hurting or "feeling tight." Therefore, always think of your best posture as your next posture. Here are some simple yet effective tips on how to counter the negative effects of sitting:

- **Take movement breaks.** A good starting rule is to get out of your seat and move at least once an hour. Leave a Post-it Note on your computer screen or set an hourly alarm on your phone to make sure you don't get stuck at your desk for hours at a time.
- **Sneak in some extra activity.** Take the stairs, park in the spot farthest away, and walk or cycle to work if you can. Make a rule to take all your calls standing or walking. Not only will your body thank you, but research also shows that meetings on the move can boost productivity and creativity by up to 60%, so this really is a win-win.
- **Check your desk setup.** Small tweaks can have a big impact. Adjust your chair and check the position and height of your screen as well as your keyboard and mouse positions.
- **Invest in a stand-up desk or a height-adjustable laptop stand.** This will allow you to adjust your working position more throughout the day. Just make sure to make it a gradual transition—you don't want to go straight from eight hours of sitting to eight hours of standing.
- **If you want to take it a step further, get a walking workstation.** Desk treadmills are gaining popularity fast and are also becoming more affordable.

Remember that stronger people are harder to kill

In addition to producing happy chemicals like endorphins and dopamine, regular exercise has been shown to increase life expectancy by up to a decade compared to a sedentary lifestyle. Exercise not only lengthens the lifespan, but also enhances your overall health. The key is to start with light activities, such as walking, and gradually intensify. Building strength and muscle mass further improves longevity and overall health. Therefore, include both cardiovascular exercise and strength training in a balanced fitness routine.

Maximize the effectiveness and sustainability of your exercise routine by working with a qualified coach or trainer who understands your goals and lifestyle. A tailored plan, rather than relying solely on the presence of an attractive Instagram profile, can help you achieve long-term success.

IMPACT

1

COMMON LEADERSHIP CHALLENGES

In today's corporate leadership world, leaders face various challenges that test their skills and strategic thinking. These challenges shape them into exceptional leaders as they use their experience and character to overcome obstacles and lead their organizations to success. We will explore some of the most common challenges faced by corporate leaders and how they navigate the complex business landscape. These are encapsulated in the ten points below:

1. **Managing Change and Uncertainty**: In a world of constant change and unpredictability, leaders have the important task of guiding their organizations through uncertain times. Hence, they should be adaptable, anticipate trends, and lead their teams toward positive outcomes.

2. **Fostering Innovation**: Leaders should create an environment that encourages new ideas and creative thinking. They can drive product innovation, embrace new ways of doing business, and find unique solutions to complex problems.
3. **Leading a Diverse Workforce**: In a globalized world, leaders often find themselves leading a diverse workforce. They need to build inclusive teams that value diversity and take advantage of unique perspectives, backgrounds, and talents within the organization.
4. **Navigating Digital Transformation**: The rapid pace of technological advancements presents both opportunities and challenges for leaders. Embracing digital transformation and leveraging emerging technologies such as artificial intelligence, automation, and data analytics are critical to staying competitive. Leaders should possess the vision to identify digital trends and strategically incorporate them into their business strategies.
5. **Building and Maintaining Strong Relationships**: Successful leaders recognize the importance of building strong relationships with stakeholders, including employees, customers, partners, and sometimes investors. Nurturing these relationships, both internal and external, helps leaders garner support, build trust, and create a robust foundation for collaboration and growth.
6. **Balancing Short-Term and Long-Term Goals**: Corporate leaders should strike a delicate balance between short-term operational demands and long-term strategic

goals. They need to allocate resources wisely, manage their time, and prioritize initiatives to ensure that the organization remains on track to achieve its long-term vision while meeting immediate objectives.

7. **Managing Risk and Uncertainty**: Risk management plays a crucial role in corporate leadership. Leaders should establish effective risk-mitigation strategies, enabling them to identify potential risks, evaluate their potential impact, and take proactive measures to minimize risk exposure while remaining agile and adaptable in the face of uncertainty.

8. **Hiring, Developing, and Retaining Top Talent**: A significant challenge leaders face is to attract, develop, and retain top talent. Building a culture of learning and growth, providing clear paths for advancement, and offering competitive compensation and benefits are vital to attracting and retaining talented individuals who will fuel the organization's success.

9. **Ethical Decision-Making**: Leaders often face ethical dilemmas. Upholding ethical standards, promoting transparency, and acting with integrity are crucial for building trust and reputation and navigating governance and social responsibility issues.

10. **Leveraging Globalization**: In a globalized world, leaders should understand and adapt to different cultures, economic conditions, and regulations. They should drive global collaborations and take advantage of international markets to expand their organization's reach and influence.

A few solutions to most problems

In addition to the top ten challenges mentioned above, there are many more, depending on the business, industry, culture, or product lifecycle. However, regardless of the challenge, there are some common strategies that can empower leaders to navigate the challenge successfully.

Firstly, embracing a growth mindset that fosters a culture of continuous learning within the organization is essential. Leaders should encourage their teams to embrace change, seek new knowledge, and develop new skills. By investing in training and development programs, leaders can equip their workforce with the right tools to adapt to evolving challenges.

Secondly, effective communication is crucial. Leaders should communicate their vision, goals, and expectations clearly to inspire and align their teams. They should promote open and transparent communication, actively listen to their employees, and provide feedback and recognition. By fostering a culture of communication, leaders can build trust, enhance collaboration, and cultivate an inclusive environment where diverse perspectives are valued.

Thirdly, problem-solving **skills** are indispensable. Leaders need to approach challenges with a strategic and analytical mindset. They should gather relevant data, conduct thorough analyses, and develop creative solutions. Decisiveness and resilience are also required to navigate unforeseen obstacles. By identifying and implementing innovative solutions, leaders can adapt their strategies effectively and lead their organizations toward success.

Fourthly, creating and nurturing strong relationships is vital in overcoming these challenges. Building and maintaining relationships with stakeholders, including employees, customers, partners, and regulators, fosters trust and collaboration. Leaders should cultivate meaningful connections, be empathetic, and actively seek feedback. By nurturing these relationships, leaders can foster a strong foundation of support and create a network of resources that can aid in overcoming various challenges.

Finally, being authentic and acting as role models for their teams are musts. Demonstrating authenticity, integrity, and ethical decision-making sets the tone for the organization's culture. By consistently embodying the values and principles they espouse, leaders inspire their teams to follow suit, fostering a culture of excellence, teamwork, and innovation.

Examples of successful leadership in the face of roadblocks

1. **Tim Cook – Managing Change and Uncertainty:**
   Tim Cook, the CEO of Apple, successfully managed the challenge of navigating change and uncertainty following the untimely death of Apple's iconic co-founder, Steve Jobs. With his steady hand and strategic mindset, Cook ensured a smooth transition and led Apple to continued success and innovation, expanding product lines and entering new

markets with transformative products such as the Apple Watch and AirPods.

2. **Virginia "Ginni" Rometty – Fostering Innovation:**
Ginni Rometty, the former CEO of IBM, exemplified the power of fostering innovation during her tenure. Rometty drove a culture of technological transformation, spearheading IBM's focus on emerging technologies such as artificial intelligence, cloud computing, and analytics. Under her leadership, IBM became a leading player in cutting-edge advancements and pioneered breakthrough initiatives like Watson, IBM's cognitive computing system.

3. **Brian Chesky – Leading a Diverse Workforce:**
Brian Chesky, the co-founder and CEO of Airbnb, led the charge in fostering diversity and inclusivity within the company. Chesky promoted inclusive hiring practices and launched initiatives to create a welcoming and supportive culture. Through these efforts, he enabled Airbnb to harness the talents and perspectives of individuals from diverse backgrounds, fostering innovation and global growth.

4. **Sundar Pichai – Navigating Digital Transformation:**
Sundar Pichai, the CEO of Google and its parent company, Alphabet, deftly led the company through the challenges of digital transformation. Pichai recognized the importance of mobile devices and successfully shifted Google's focus toward mobile and cloud computing. Under his leadership, Google expanded its product offerings and achieved tremendous success, further solidifying its status as a technology powerhouse.

COMMON LEADERSHIP CHALLENGES

5. **Mary Dillon – Building and Maintaining Strong Relationships:**
   Mary Dillon, the CEO of Ulta Beauty, built and maintained strong relationships to propel the company's success. She fostered a customer-centric culture and built strong partnerships with beauty brands, enhancing the customer experience and increasing the company's market share. Her relationship-focused approach helped Ulta Beauty become a leading beauty retailer in the United States.
6. **Bernard J. Tyson – Balancing Short-Term and Long-Term Goals:**
   Bernard J. Tyson, the former CEO of Kaiser Permanente, successfully balanced short-term and long-term goals by implementing a holistic approach focused on delivering immediate patient care while promoting preventive care and community health initiatives. Tyson's leadership forged a path toward sustainable healthcare practices that addressed both immediate needs and long-term societal impact.
7. **Mark Benioff – Developing and Retaining Top Talent:**
   Mark Benioff, the CEO of Salesforce, is known for his focus on developing and retaining top talent. He emphasizes continuous learning, career growth, and cultivating a culture of purpose and giving back. Under Benioff's leadership, Salesforce became renowned as a desirable workplace and a pioneer in philanthropy, attracting and retaining a group of talented professionals who embodied the company's values.

8. **Elon Musk – Leveraging Globalization:**
   Elon Musk, the CEO of Tesla and SpaceX, has emerged as a visionary leader adept at leveraging globalization. He has expanded his companies' reach beyond domestic markets, establishing manufacturing plants, research and development centers, and satellite projects in various countries. Musk's ability to navigate cultural complexities, regulatory landscapes, and global supply chains has enabled Tesla and SpaceX to thrive on a global scale. His charismatic leadership and innovative mindset have revolutionized the automotive and space industries, earning him global recognition and admiration.

2

LEADERSHIP IN THE DIGITAL ERA

The world today is undergoing rapid disruption and digital transformation, affecting almost every aspect of our daily lives. The business environment is in constant flux, demanding a shift in the approach organizations adopt to cope with these changes. This evolution demands a transformative leadership style adaptable to futuristic methods for enabling new strategies and best practices to keep abreast of today's shifting patterns. Here are some key traits that reflect the evolving nature of leadership in the digital age:

1. **Innovation**: Leaders should facilitate and promote innovation within their organizations to adjust to constantly shifting technological advancements. Here, I am not talking only about new technologies. Innovation could happen

in every part of the business and every department. Leaders should encourage individuals to develop and share creative ideas. I remember my manager in my first job asking me to do a task in a certain way that would have taken me about two weeks to complete. It was a boring Excel sheet to calculate a bonus and profit share payout for the entire population of the bank with over 50 branches. I went on Google and tried to find a faster way of doing it with some formulae or functions. There was no Power BI or AI at that time. When I found a way, I went back to him excited to tell him I had finished the task well before the deadline. He looked at me and told me that it was impossible. He tried to find a mistake in all the sheets but couldn't. Then he asked me why I hadn't used the way he had explained to me. I told him that I thought this would be faster. His response was, "I have been the manager for nine years. You should follow the way I ask you to follow." I resigned a few days later because this was not the leader or culture that inspired me.

2. **Intentional engagement**: Leaders should encourage platforms for cross-functional communication and inspirational ideas to challenge organizational obstacles. Whether you are leading a small or large organization, create programs where you get your employees' thoughts about various parts of their roles and the business. It could be a monthly or quarterly survey of new ideas they might think of. Then put people in teams to work on these ideas. Ideally, bring people from different teams to work together on these initiatives. These initiatives could be new ideas or new ways to solve existing challenges. As a leader, you

don't have to be the one solving all the problems. Tap into every team member's background to come up with the best solutions.

3. **Customer orientation**: Organizations are now placing increasing importance on being customer-centric. Leaders should anticipate shifts in customer trends through critical strategic assessments, scrutinizing and aligning cross-functional business units accordingly toward better customer-experience perceptions in return for sustainable organizational growth patterns. If customer-centricity is not part of your core values, you might need to consider re-evaluating your values. Customers always have to be at the center of every decision you make. One of the favorite techniques to remind us of customers in all meetings is to keep an empty seat in every meeting you lead. This seat represents your customer. Think of what the customer would be happy and unhappy about in your meeting. When you take your team's opinions during the meeting, ask them and yourself what the customer would feel about your ideas. Combine the outcome with all the quantitative and qualitative feedback you receive from the customers through surveys and all interactions.

4. **Technological fluency**: Today's leaders need fluency in advanced technology and its implications for their organization. Understanding newer digital tools and how they function can ensure skilled development toward better productivity and expense containment with the rise of AI and all its tools. If you do not leverage its speed, accuracy, and efficiency, you might be missing ways to streamline your

work, improve productivity, and, eventually, the customer experience. There are many products out there that are still premature, and there are others that can help you and your team be more efficient, such as ChatGPT 4.0, Tomeapp.com for presentations, Fireflies AI for meeting notes, Stockimg AI and Midjourney AI for creating images, and many more apps and websites that can increase your productivity.

5. **Agility**: Leaders today should encourage organizational agility and innovation, enabling quick adjustment and embracing organizational fluidity amidst disruptive changes. Strategic assessments focus on replacing stagnant practices with fluid guidelines. This could be difficult to achieve in large organizations and requires careful handling. However, many organizations are shifting today to a more decentralized structure to react to the market faster than the competition.

Leveraging technology as a leader

In the age of rapid digital transformation, technology has become increasingly important in leadership roles. To stay ahead of the competition, leaders need to acknowledge technological shifts, adapt quickly to new developments, and identify new opportunities for innovation. Technology has become a critical tool in enhancing overall business performance and customer satisfaction and assisting with formulating strategies. Effective technology-leveraging leadership can streamline and accelerate business procedures, tasks, decision-making, and outcomes. Let me share some ways in which you can leverage technology and stay current with emerging trends:

1. **Pursue continuous learning:** Staying informed regarding advanced tech trends provides invaluable information and ensures leaders retain the latest information. Activities like online conferences, readings, podcasts, webinars, and knowledge-sharing forums are notable ways of augmenting technical knowledge regularly and keeping up-to-the-minute regarding dynamic tech trends and industry standards. I spend a lot of time on the road or flying, so podcasts are my go-to source of information. I try to find reliable sources such as Andrew Huberman, Steve Barlett, Chris Williamson, and Tim Ferris, among others. In many organizations, teams start their meetings with 15 minutes of knowledge sharing. Each team member leads this part and shares any new or interesting information relevant to the team's line of work. This way, you take your first steps to creating a learning organization.
2. **Foster a tech-oriented culture:** Leadership should build a culture that embraces new technology investments that look like they will acquire widespread acceptance and enhance productivity, sustainability, and professional innovations. Unfortunately, it is difficult in today's world to survive for long without being tech-savvy. If you are still uncomfortable with talking about and learning all the new technology coming up, find a tech mentor or a "buddy"

who can guide you through the first steps. Once you see the value it brings to your work, you will never stop learning.

3. **Become a data-informed decision-maker**: Today's leaders need to be data-informed decision-makers, leveraging the power of sophisticated data analytics software while analyzing iterative processes and performance statistics in real time, gathering valuable feedback. This yields a deeper comprehension of the marketplace or customer behaviors regarding processes. Leaders could have gotten away with making decisions without the support of data in the past because the competition was doing the same. However, today's competition is leveraging all the data they can get in their daily decisions. If you as a leader are not doing the same, you will fall behind sooner than you think.

Technology at the heart of transformation

Digital transformation is an essential aspect of modern business, with technology playing a central role in many successful companies. These transformations have revitalized several businesses. Let's take a look at some case studies of leaders in companies adapting to digital transformation and putting technology at the heart of their transformation journey.

1. **Jeff Bezos (Founder and former CEO of Amazon)**: Bezos revolutionized the retail industry by leveraging technology

to build Amazon into an e-commerce giant. His vision and strategic use of technology have enabled the company to deliver exceptional customer experiences, disrupt traditional retail models, and diversify into various sectors, including cloud computing and entertainment.

2. **Elon Musk (CEO of Tesla and SpaceX)**: Musk's leadership has transformed the automotive and aerospace industries. With Tesla, he has pioneered electric vehicles and sustainable energy solutions, while SpaceX has revolutionized space exploration. Musk's visionary use of technology has led to market disruption, driving innovation and remarkable growth.

3. **Shantanu Narayen (CEO of Adobe Systems)**: Narayen's leadership has shifted Adobe's focus from a traditional software company to a cloud-based digital experiences provider. By embracing data analytics, AI, and the subscription model, he successfully reinvented Adobe's business model, delivering exceptional financial results and driving market leadership.

4. **Ginni Rometty (Former CEO of IBM)**: Rometty transformed IBM by leveraging technology such as cognitive computing and cloud services. Her strategic vision fueled IBM's investments in emerging technologies, inspiring a shift toward AI-driven solutions and hybrid cloud offerings, which have helped the organization stay ahead in a highly competitive market.

5. **Brian Halligan and Dharmesh Shah (Co-founders of HubSpot)**: Halligan and Shah pioneered inbound marketing with HubSpot, a software platform that integrates

inbound marketing, sales, and customer service. Their technology-driven approach to marketing has empowered companies worldwide to attract customers organically, deliver personalized experiences, and achieve remarkable business growth.

6. **Reed Hastings (Co-founder and CEO of Netflix)**: Hastings transformed the entertainment industry by ushering in the streaming era through Netflix. By leveraging technology and data analytics, he disrupted traditional television models, enabling consumers to stream content on demand. Hastings' foresight and innovation have not only driven exceptional business results, but also revolutionized how people consume entertainment.

3

CULTIVATING GROWTH MINDSETS TO UNLOCK HIGH-PERFORMANCE TEAMS

While talking to a friend and colleague in one of the largest multinational oil/gas companies, where he is a global operations leader, I asked how he manages work–life balance with the 24/7 operation and customer needs. He told me that it had taken him time to build a high-performing team, but once he'd done that, he was able to manage the business from his vacation house in Europe.

One of a leader's principal responsibilities is to build a high-performing team. However, doing so requires an environment conducive to collaboration, understanding the challenges, and self-assessing failures. Successful leaders looking to establish a growth mindset in their teams should communicate growth-oriented messages, identify the key strengths and limitations of individual team members, identify opportunities for development, and align key performance indicators with visionary goals.

Hiring employees based on strengths and talent and investing in their development can foster innovation within the team, and the ability of each member to contribute to progress is fundamental. Additionally, teams are more apt to improve through feedback—it is a critical tool for leaders aiming to develop comprehensive strategies that harbor innovation and improvement. There should be a clear and concise expansion framework aimed at getting key performance indicators (KPIs) aligned with organizational objectives that cascade through micro-teams and individuals.

Identifying individual strengths in a team with a detailed focus on unique personality dynamics ensures leaders can optimally apply these strengths to achieve success for the whole team. These factors, among others, are key drivers in active learning. Painting a picture of upward mobility for dedicated team members has the benefit of cultivating personnel who wholly own the responsibility of creating their own goals and contribute to the growth and development of the company, ultimately driving success both individually and collectively.

Growth mindset

The term "growth mindset" has become a buzzword. But what does it really mean? It refers to a core set of beliefs that individuals and organizations possess that suggest a vast part of complex endowments can be established through innovative efforts, grit, dedication, and upskilling. According to Carol Dweck, a psychologist from Stanford University whose work dominates the space, a growth mindset involves trusting in one's unseen ability to learn and viewing obstacles not as limitations, but as opportunities for personal shift and innovation. A growth mindset emphasizes that anything can be transformed—including innate traits and learned abilities. It actively reaches out and creates a profound environment to foster learning and adaptability for individuals and organizations alike.

It sounds intuitive, right? But how many leaders do you know who do not accept feedback or constructive criticism? People with a growth mindset tend to perceive criticism as an opportunity to grow, not a sign of failure. Individuals with a growth mindset rely on constructive feedback from peers or supervisors to create personal development blueprints and pathways. Consequently, a growth mindset allows individuals and teams to be more receptive, thus opening up higher capability and unlocking complexity via agile growth sessions. A growth mindset is fast becoming a tool for entrepreneurs, corporations, and people looking to establish working habits that define long-term success.

Hiring for a growth mindset

If you, as a leader, get the chance to hire someone, consider yourself very lucky. Mostly, you have to work with what you've got. Working with an inherited team could be very challenging for several reasons, especially if there are different power dynamics, skill gaps, and personality clashes. But we also need to agree that recruiting individuals who already have a growth mindset can be daunting for leaders. To ensure that a company has employees who are growth-mindset inclined, recruitment strategies put an emphasis on establishing an environment and value system that encourages authenticity and self-awareness while featuring advertising and promotional strategies for the job opening.

Many leaders are not involved in job postings. HR or talent acquisition works on the job description and posting. If done right, leaders need to be involved in the job postings that convey the company's value systems and culture, articulating the nature of priorities driving recruitment efforts, expected ideals, and shared objectives among the team. Aligning requisites and prerequisites with the growth mindset policy addresses both personality attributes and required capabilities. It is not easy to make time for all of this. Business pressure is never easy. However, a strong HR team should be able to help you with it.

An important component of recruiting individuals for a growth-favoring culture involves using competency assessments when evaluating potential personnel. Assessments are tools to measure a candidate's capacity to think, show initiative and innovation, problem-solve, and display a passion for self-discovery and development. Such assessments determine how these factors align with the company's value system. Most organizations have a competencies model with a clear definition of competency and behavioral indicators to help you identify what good looks like. Go ask your HR team or design a simple model to help you paint a picture of what you are looking for so you can recognize it when you see it. Having a clear competencies model and standard approach for interviewing candidates will increase the probability of hiring the right person and help reduce biases, inconsistencies, and many other assessment pitfalls.

This is what a basic competency should look like. Visit www.thecorporateoffical.com to get help in identifying key competencies for assessing internal and external talents.

Competency Name: DECISION-MAKING

Definition: Identifying and understanding problems; choosing an effective course of action and/or developing appropriate solutions; taking action that is consistent with available facts.

Behavioral indicators

- Identifies problems.
- Gathers information.
- Generates a solution.
- Clarifies the action needed.
- Commits to action.

Strategies to sustain high performance

1. **Foster a shared vision**: A shared vision is a compelling and inspiring goal that rallies team members around a common purpose. When leaders articulate a clear vision,

they give their teams a sense of direction and purpose. Aligning individual goals and tasks with the broader team objectives creates cohesion and motivation. This strategy is supported by various management theories, including the Transformational Leadership theory proposed by James MacGregor Burns.

2. **Set challenging goals**: Challenging goals push team members beyond their comfort zone and get them to strive for exceptional performance. By setting specific, measurable, attainable, relevant, and time-bound (SMART) goals, leaders motivate their team members and promote personal growth.
3. **Promote trust and psychological safety**: Trust and psychological safety are crucial for fostering collaboration, innovation, and risk-taking within a team. Leaders can create a safe and supportive environment by allowing open communication, encouraging healthy conflict resolution, and valuing diverse opinions. The concept of psychological safety was introduced by Amy Edmondson.
4. **Enhance communication**: Effective communication is fundamental to team success. Leaders can promote communication by establishing open channels, encouraging active listening, providing timely feedback, and facilitating effective meetings. Studies in organizational communication by Amanda J. Sharkey and other researchers provide guidance on enhancing communication within teams.
5. **Build a diverse team**: A diverse team brings together individuals with unique perspectives, skills, and experience. Such diversity fosters creativity, innovation, and

problem-solving skills. Leaders can recruit diverse candidates, promote inclusivity, and leverage the benefits of diverse thinking and collaboration. Numerous studies on diversity, inclusion, and team performance support this strategy.

6. **Promote accountability**: Clearly defining roles, responsibilities, and expectations is essential to foster accountability within a team. Leaders can establish performance metrics, track progress, and hold individuals responsible for their contributions. This approach aligns with concepts from performance management and organizational behavior literature.

7. **Provide continuous learning opportunities**: *Harvard Business Review* has identified progress as one of the key motivators in the workplace. So, to sustain a high-performing team, leaders should invest in the development of their members. Offering training, mentorship programs, and developmental opportunities will help team members enhance their skills, knowledge, and expertise. This aligns with the concept of continuous learning and development from the human resource management literature.

8. **Recognize and reward excellence**: Recognizing and rewarding individual and team achievements not only boosts motivation, but also reinforces a culture of high performance. Leaders can do so through verbal praise, public recognition, promotions, bonuses, and other forms of rewards and incentives.

9. **Encourage collaboration and teamwork**: Collaboration and teamwork are essential for synchronizing efforts,

sharing knowledge, and achieving collective goals. Leaders can foster collaboration by creating opportunities for joint decision-making—in this way, encouraging cross-functional cooperation and valuing collective achievements.
10. **Empower and delegate**: Empowering team members by delegating authority and autonomy promotes a sense of ownership and responsibility. Leaders should trust their team members' competence, provide them with decision-making authority, and allow them to utilize their expertise.

The dark side of high-performing teams

1. **Burnout**: High-performing teams often work at a fast pace with ambitious goals. The drive for excellence and constant pressure to deliver can increase the risk of burnout among team members.
2. **Workload Imbalance**: In pursuit of exceptional performance, team members with higher abilities or stronger skills may take on more responsibilities, leading to an imbalance in workload distribution.
3. **Strained Relationships**: The desire to achieve high performance can create a demanding and competitive environment, leading to strained relationships between team members if not properly managed. Collaboration and teamwork may suffer as a result.

4. **Dunning–Kruger Effect**: This is the name given to a cognitive bias that makes people think they are smarter than they are. People who suffer from it lack the ability to assess the skill they believe they have, leading them to assume they actually have this particular skill. The biggest issue is that someone who was successful in the past could also suffer from the Dunning–Kruger Effect—their prior success makes them think they still are.

Embrace experimentation and risk-taking as a means of innovation and growth

Promoting a "fail fast" strategy can stimulate innovation in a team. By embracing this approach, leaders create a culture wherein taking risks and experimenting with new ideas is not only accepted but encouraged. The fail-fast strategy emphasizes learning from failures and quickly adapting to find solutions. It allows team members to test ideas, gather feedback, and make necessary adjustments or pivot if the initial approach does not yield desired results. This mindset not only fosters creativity and unconventional thinking but also eliminates the fear of failure, which can often stifle innovation. It enables team members to learn from their mistakes, iterate, and continuously improve, leading ultimately to breakthrough ideas and innovative solutions that can drive high performance and success. In summary, by promoting a fail-fast strategy, leaders set the stage for an environment that prioritizes innovation, resilience, and agility, empowering their teams to explore new possibilities and achieve exceptional results.

Celebrating accomplishments and giving credit where credit is due

Celebrating team success and giving credit where it's due is not only important but essential for building a positive and high-performing team culture. Recognizing and celebrating success not only boosts morale but also reinforces a sense of accomplishment and pride among team members. It highlights the hard work, dedication, and achievements of individuals and the collective efforts of the team. By acknowledging and appreciating their contributions, leaders inspire and motivate team members to continue striving for excellence.

Giving credit where it's due builds trust and fosters a supportive environment. When leaders publicly recognize and attribute success to specific team members, it establishes a culture of fairness and transparency. This practice demonstrates that individual efforts are seen, valued, and rewarded. When team members feel acknowledged and appreciated, it enhances their commitment to the team's goals and encourages collaboration and positive relationships.

4

TRANSFORMING CULTURE, EMPOWERING TEAMS

"Culture is not just one aspect of the game—it is the game."

— Lou Gerstner

Have you heard the saying, "Culture eats strategy for breakfast?" A positive organizational culture is critical to a company's success. "Organizational culture" refers to the shared values, beliefs, and behaviors that define how a company's employees interact with each other and the wider world. A positive organizational culture can improve everything from employee engagement to productivity to innovation—all of which contribute to improved overall performance. And here, I am talking about the *real* culture lived every day by employees and leaders, not what the company's career portal advertises.

Why is this so important? Well, a good organizational culture can foster a sense of trust between employees and managers, which leads to better collaboration and a work environment where people aren't afraid to share ideas or ask questions. It can also build brand loyalty among consumers who want to support companies with values that align with their own. A strong culture can also help attract and retain top talent, which is critical for any organization looking to grow and succeed.

So, it's clear that organizational culture is crucial for today's businesses. Building that culture takes time and effort, as it needs to be intentionally cultivated and reinforced. But in the long run, investing in a strong organizational culture is proven to be worth it. The sooner you get started working to nurture and define your company's culture, the better off you'll be.

The role of leadership in shaping and transforming organizational culture

Leadership plays a crucial role in determining and shaping organizational culture. It's not just about the skills, expertise, and functional know-how of leaders—effective leaders also embody a strong set of values and behaviors that reflect and reinforce their organization's culture. In order to create and promote a positive organizational culture, leaders need to provide a vision that can inspire and motivate employees. By modeling the behaviors they want to promote, communicating effectively, and providing opportunities for employees to grow and develop, leaders can create an environment that fosters open communication and collaboration, creativity and innovation, inclusivity and diversity, and a focus on achieving shared goals.

Moreover, leadership is not only about maintaining the status quo of an organization's culture. It's also about driving desired change. In order to transform an organization's culture positively, leaders need to be willing to recognize the need for change and take risks. This means creating opportunities for dialogue, listening to feedback and concerns, and taking the time to identify areas where improvement is needed. Sometimes it takes a lot of courage to admit that you need to look to your employees and listen to what they have to say. Most of the time, what they have to say is not very pleasant, especially when leaders have been shying away from assessing their culture for a long time.

Remember, if your business is going through a transformation, whether it is a digital transformation, a merger, an acquisition, or any other (which is inevitable for any business's survival in the 21st century), you need to address your cultural readiness as a priority. Several studies have shown that 70% of change initiatives fail for cultural reasons.

Transforming a company's culture is no easy task, but leaders who are committed and responsive to feedback from all levels of the organization, while staying true to their values and vision, can effect real change.

Cultural diagnosis

Diagnosing and measuring your organization's culture is critical to understanding what aspects of it need to be improved or reinforced. But where do you start? One way is to survey employees and managers about their perceptions and experiences in the workplace. This can be done through anonymous surveys, focus groups, and interviews. You can also analyze company data to identify patterns and trends, such as employee turnover rates or customer feedback. It is worth noting that surveys will not show you the full truth; many factors could interfere with the survey, such as its timing. It might occur close to a layoff wave, a merit cycle, or another event that could influence employees' responses. I always suggest following up with sessions and interviews conducted by a third party or a trusted HR partner to maintain anonymity.

Another approach is to use cultural diagnostics tools specifically developed to measure organizational culture. These tools can be very helpful in providing a more detailed and comprehensive view of your culture beyond what might be discernable through surveys or secondary data analysis. Examples of these tools include the Organizational Culture Assessment Instrument (OCAI), Competing Values Framework (CVF), and Denison Organizational Culture Survey (DOCS).

Once you have a solid understanding of your organization's culture, you can use this information to make data-driven decisions that will help shape and improve your culture. For instance, if your team's collaboration needs improvement, you can use insights from your survey data to find ways to align collaboration in the right direction. With improved cultural awareness, you can build a roadmap of initiatives tailored to your unique context and targeted at improving your organization's culture in meaningful ways.

Strategies for identifying areas of improvement and opportunities for change

Once you have obtained measurements for your organization's culture and diagnosed potential areas for improvement, the next step is to build effective strategies for change. It is important to pinpoint specific areas where change is required and then design a clear roadmap complete with set goals and objectives. You should also consider creating a change management team and encouraging employee involvement with (and dedication to) goals that integrate teamwork. You can assign a leader to champion one of the improvement areas and lead a team to build a strategy for improvement.

Furthermore, you can build strategies to identify opportunities for change by working on your team's core values with a non-judgmental and open mindset. Focus on rebuilding purpose, legacy, and success with an emphasis on teamwork, alignment, and engagement. Create policies that embrace diversity, foster respect, enhance creativity, and encourage employees' professional growth. Develop a winning culture that builds leadership through inspiring your team to place priority on strengthening its values and aligning with the company's mission. Evaluate the outcomes and strive to improve regularly with a commitment to transparency, honesty, and clear communication.

Finally, to create sustainable and effective change, encourage transparency, accountability, and consistent communication. Effective communication is achieved by understanding how individuals are either uplifted or threatened by change and what responses will be helpful in navigating fluctuations within your organization. The implemented strategy should be tailored to respond appropriately to negative feedback. Successful change demands a strong atmosphere of honesty, transparency, and learning so that all members of your team take ownership of the changes that affect them.

Here are some examples of the most common cultural values in most organizations. If your organization and team have not yet identified them, work with them on creating a cultural values framework consisting of less than ten values, with their description and behavioral indicators. They have to be simple and clear for employees to follow.

Agility – Authenticity – Collaboration – Creativity – Customer focus – Dedication – Diversity and inclusion – Empathy – Empowerment – Ethics – Excellence – Experimentation – Flexibility – Growth mindset – Humility – Innovation – Learning – Open-mindedness – Ownership – Passion – Persuasion – Quality – Respect – Results orientation – Risk-taking – Safety – Service to others –

Social responsibility – Stewardship – Sustainability – Teamwork – Transparency – Trustworthiness – Winning mentality – Work-life balance – Work ethic – Adaptability – Accountability – Courage – Fun

Best practices for developing a positive culture

To foster a culture that promotes innovation, leaders should encourage employees to share their ideas and approaches to solving problems. They should create an environment that values experimentation and risk-taking. Such an environment promotes the free flow of ideas without fear of retribution. Leaders should provide team members with the resources and support they need to develop and implement their innovative solutions. They should recognize and reward employees who come up with innovative ideas that lead to positive organizational impact—this will foster a culture of creativity. Leaders also need to acquire a level of maturity before they can deal with employees who respectfully challenge the status quo. You might have heard leaders say they promote innovation, but then seen them shut people down whenever they come up with an idea.

Reward and recognition programs help foster a culture of positive reinforcement to celebrate the successes of both individuals and teams. This includes awards and company-wide recognition, or maybe a simple acknowledgment might be enough. Developing recognition programs that celebrate individuals' achievements, expertise, or accomplishments further motivates other team members to learn and meet ambitious objectives. Fostering a culture of thankfulness helps the employees feel appreciated and energized, leading to increased employee satisfaction.

Establishing teamwork best practices can promote a positive culture within employees and, in turn, enhance business results. Creating opportunities for team-building events, acknowledging milestones and accomplishments, and encouraging cooperation are the building blocks of healthy teamwork.

Leaders should encourage transparent, open communications that prioritize building an environment where feedback is welcome. By establishing reliable feedback mechanisms, leaders can gain insight into employee needs and opinions, leadership effectiveness, and company direction. Leaders can then follow up with specific strategies to bridge gaps and improve performance.

Leaders should set high-performance expectations and mission statements that underscore the importance of excellent performance in their target areas. They should also be clear about what productivity involves and establish SMART goals that help employees focus on understanding their job responsibilities that align with company objectives. One of the companies I know calls this "Flawless Execution"—no pressure for everyone who works there!

Examples of what happens when you misalign strategy with culture

The misalignment of cultural strategy with business transformation initiatives can lead to significant negative consequences. Here are two examples of where an organization failed to align its cultural strategy with its business transformation:

1. In August 2011, a tech hardware multinational announced it would be discontinuing its personal computers division. Later, in November 2012, it wrote down the division for one-third of its value, costing billions and facing significant public relations damage. Furthermore, the company found it challenging to execute transitions due to disparities in culture between it and a software company it had acquired in 2011. The result of misalignments reduced employee morale and led to job cuts, lawsuits, and failed critical operations. It costs billions to restore the losses.
2. A giant multinational aimed to redefine its decision-making authority and rethink employees' roles and expectations. The CEO cut costs in key business units, making employees feel unvalued and undervalued. Indeed, shortly afterward allegations of fraud and scandals involving ballooning liabilities emerged, including an inquiry into its communications unit. The industrial company had a crisis of culture and risk-taking with downward spiraling profits, resulting in one of the worst downhill runs in its history.

Consequently, cultural misalignment created chaos and lost long-term shareholder value and credibility.

The success of business initiatives depends on the values, beliefs, and supportive actions that create a sustainable culture. Organizational cultural misalignments produce symptoms far beyond behavioral and operational inconsistencies. These may lead to low morale, disengagement, poor retention, data breaches, and ethical malfunctions, damaging the reliability of critical processes and strategic objectives.

Keeping your finger on the pulse

Cultural change is critical, but the effort needs more than an implementation strategy and a contingency plan. Leaders who initiate cultural changes need appropriate management, and measurement should occur continuously to assess the effectiveness of the changes. To maintain good results and promote cultural sustainability, reinforcement of cultural shifts is necessary.

Continuous reinforcement of cultural change is crucial to sustaining changes over a long period. Repeated messages through town hall meetings, webinars, work sessions, and mentorship forums keep people thinking and contextualize behaviors and principles to embody these strategies, approaches, and objectives. The goal is to avoid the regression of cultural shifts and retain constant advocacy. Conducting surveys, feedback analysis, and sentiment analysis can help pinpoint the focus areas for reinforcement.

Leaders also need to ensure that key measures are put in place that align with the core value systems transforming their culture. Metrics could include improved revenue, more effective employee performance, and higher customer satisfaction. Additionally, companies could track high- and low-performing processes and map them on a slope. Ensuring that the measurement framework continuously aligns with business strategy and culture is critical to positive and informed decision-making by top executives.

It is essential to reinforce and measure cultural change, so that the organization keeps up with the times, including competition, challenges, technological disruptions, and socio-economic factors—thus ensuring organizations are continuously learning and adapting. An agile organization requires a paradigm shift toward the growth mindset of a learning culture resilient to globalization, new economic formats, and different generational values. Regular training sessions and implementation periods that constructively progress key strategic imperatives are essential methods to adopt.

Case studies of companies that have successfully transformed their cultures

Transforming an organizational culture might seem like a daunting task, but many companies have successfully taken the initiative to change by adopting the best business strategies and initiatives. Here are four examples of companies that have transformed their cultures positively:

1. **Microsoft** reimagined its culture with new business approaches and employee well-being programs, among other collaborations. Under the leadership of CEO Satya Nadella, the organization embraced empathy as a foundation for diverse specialized thinking, broad-range goal orientation, and an ongoing learning culture. The new vision for Microsoft aims to empower every organization and person to achieve more through products, platforms, and services that allow teams anywhere to collaborate in more creative and intelligent ways.
2. **Netflix** underwent a significant shift in how it was run when it introduced the "culture deck", a comprehensive corporate culture management guide. The culture deck outlines the organization's tactics for incorporation and integrates an evaluation process that continues to improve and evolve its cultural profile. The culture embeds the acceleration of live streaming services toward personalized video-on-demand services and a continual assessment of

media consumption patterns that connect more profound data insights to emerging democratizing entertainment markets.
3. **Apple** reimagined its brand strategy, first under Steve Jobs' leadership, positioning the company as a product and service superpower. Secondly, innovations, product diversity, and a practical understanding of how to build a passionate, considerate, and highly creative workforce enabled the company's backbone to empower consumers' lives and product ownership.
4. **Starbucks** embarked on a cultural change in 2008 that centered on a new employee partnership and employee satisfaction program. It built unions and empowered employees by providing healthcare and education. It also supported direct sourcing channels to coffee farmers and improved diversity in recruitment. Led by ethics and economic sustainability, it helped build staff camaraderie, leading to an enormous expansion of operations in emerging markets.

5

NAVIGATING CORPORATE POLITICS WITH INTEGRITY AND PURPOSE

Politics is often associated with shady, crafty, dirty, manipulative, behind-the-scenes tactics and behaviors that serve an individual's or a group's self-interest. But being politically savvy does not mean being any of those things.

You have probably heard leaders say they don't like to be involved in their organization's politics. Well, everyone in an organization is involved in corporate politics in one way or another—politics and leadership in the corporate world are inextricably linked. The political climate of an organization has a significant impact on the effectiveness of its leaders and, ultimately, the organization's success. In some organizations, politics is a tool to manipulate and wield power, with little regard for how stakeholders are affected. On the other hand, politics can be beneficial when leaders use it to facilitate collaboration, communicate well, and make sound decisions.

With the ongoing change that organizations go through, leaders need to navigate different interests and agendas among stakeholders, often with limited resources. Understanding how political forces can influence decision-making enables a leader to recognize and navigate those interests, build consensus, and make sound, informed decisions.

Politics can also significantly influence the performance of an organization. Leaders who understand and leverage political forces create a positive culture of open communication and feedback, leading to increased employee engagement, which, in turn, fosters innovation and business initiatives.

The research on mastering politics indicates that leaders who develop effective political skills are in a better position to influence decision-making and collaboration in high-stakes situations. These skills include building coalitions with stakeholders, using influence and persuasion to negotiate positions, grappling, understanding the organization's systems and how work gets done, and embracing change management when necessary.

Understanding inherent power structures and how they affect decision-making

Understanding power structures in organizations is critical for a corporate leader to make informed decisions and influence others. Leaders who do not grasp power structures may have difficulty advancing their initiatives or may encounter resistance from opposing forces. This is because power structures are not always formal and can operate in subtle ways, such as less obvious social influences that can leave a leader in a position of less power or influence. Therefore, understanding the informal power structures is crucial for leaders to navigate an organization easily. The next time you are in a meeting room discussing a critical business topic and facing a problem, look at where everyone is looking in the room. Is it at the official leader or someone else?

One way that leaders can understand power structures in their organization is by identifying stakeholder interests, goals, and alliances and continuously being on the lookout for signs of informal influence within their organization. Through a better understanding and careful observation, leaders may identify which stakeholders are most invested in specific outcomes, allowing them to better anticipate resistance, gain support and influence from others, and navigate operations more effectively.

A second important consideration is how to use power structures to support change or foster new initiatives. Effective leaders capitalize on informal power structures within the organization to build support for their ideas by identifying critical stakeholders who can help shape decisions essential to the outlined vision. They form alliances and leverage communication and vision to build a sense of inspired action.

A third aspect is how leaders deal with potential power struggles within their departments. Leaders should ensure that when distributing power, duties, responsibilities, and carrying out administrative practices that there are no clashes of egos or ideas, or power struggles among themselves, team members, or co-workers. The skills of decision-making—active listening, empathic communication, negotiation, and problem-solving—are powerful means of developing shared goals and mutual respect.

Power structures are present in all organizations, and understanding the character of the structures and the influencing factors of key stakeholders is a critical component of effective leadership and can have significant effects on organizational performance.

Building alliances

Building alliances, coalitions, and support networks is essential for a leader's success, as it can help a leader navigate complex organizational ecosystems, gain support, and facilitate change. Leaders need to identify key stakeholders and seek their support to advance their initiatives, create new practices and legislative programs, or resolve key problems affecting organizational goals. These stakeholders could be peers, direct reports, or managers.

Before discussing *how* to do it, I would like to remind you *when* and *who* you need to prioritize building a relationship. While I favor building strong relationships with everyone—your job becomes so much easier when you have strong relationships with all the people you work with—there are key groups that you should not miss. First, do not wait until there is a problem before finding out whom you need to know to solve it. You need to be ahead of the problem. The three most important groups of people you need to build a relationship with are the ones that affect your current job, your future jobs, and people who could give you insights into the organization that might not necessarily be important for performing today's job. Do not fall into the trap of building a relationship with a stakeholder because you have a problem to solve or building relationships only with the people you like and like you. Build relationships with people who are unlike you, and then solve the problem while you already have a strong relationship with them. Remember, authenticity is key. If you intend to build relationships only to sway decisions when needed, it will be obvious. However, if you do it out of empathy, trust, and collaboration toward a common goal, you will come across as genuine and trustworthy.

Now let's talk about the *how*. For peers and management, you might use different strategies from the ones you would normally use with direct reports. However, no matter what the stakeholder group is, start with **trust**. Trust is the foundation of any successful alliance. Foster open and honest communication, follow through on commitments, and maintain confidentiality when necessary. In his book *Crucial Conversations*, Kerry Patterson categorized trust into four pillars. The first one is **reliability**: does the person do what they say they do? The second one is **motive**: Are both of your reasonings for doing something aligned? The third pillar is **transparency**: Is the person communicating enough and sharing all the relevant information or keeping stakeholders in the dark? The fourth is **capability**: Do you trust that this person can do what they should be doing? If you understand these four pillars, you can apply them to any relationship you have.

Another way (which could be more important in some organizations than others) is to **network** by attending industry events, conferences, and social gatherings to meet and connect with influential individuals, actively engaging in conversations and showing genuine interest in others. You need to build a wide network that can provide support at various levels within the organization. While this could be draining and hard work for some more than others, especially introverts, I believe if you genuinely care about the organization and the industry you are working in, it will come naturally to you—maybe one-on-one instead of a bigger group setting.

One of my favorite ways to get to know people in other geographies and functions is to **collaborate** on joint projects or initiatives with others in the organization. Working cooperatively with peers and management helps build mutual trust and a sense of shared purpose. Successful collaboration often leads to future alliances and stronger support networks.

Sharing credit is a very important leadership trait. Everyone dislikes those who take credit for the work they haven't done or fail to mention the people who put their sweat into projects. Acknowledge the contributions of others and publicly recognize their achievements. Sharing credit for collective success helps foster camaraderie and encourages others to support and collaborate with you.

As for your team members, the first strategy is to **cultivate loyalty** through transparency and mutual respect, recognizing the goals and challenges of team members. Leaders should create an atmosphere of open communication, transparency, and mutual respect where team members feel empowered to share their opinions, goals, and ideas. Listening actively and empathizing within relationships helps cultivate respect and trust across the organization and creates a better communicative framework for successful reach.

The second strategy is to **empower team members** by providing them with the necessary resources, autonomy, and support to develop, grow, and prosper. Leaders who encourage exploration, autonomy, and flexibility feel empowered and that their agency is appreciated. Empowering team members with talent investments, giving constructive feedback, and delegating missions to subordinates to drive autonomously are great strategies to build trust in the relationships and increase productivity within team members, building alliances and coalitions.

The third strategy is to **leverage new technology** to build new social networks and platforms to initiate connection and collaboration. Technologies like interactive virtual meetings, social media platforms to get acquainted, initiatives or collaborations with workers in real life, and virtual game events build essential trust among employees, helping them build kinships and increase communication and openness within a workspace.

Managing conflicting demands from different interest groups

This could be a normal day for you as a leader, especially in matrix-based organizational structures. You have to deliver long-term results without missing your short-term quarterly targets. Then you need to sell some new strategic products and services without reducing the core product sales. You need to produce high-quality products and services at relatively low prices. Then, obviously, you need to expand and grow without necessarily having additional resources and maintain a work–life balance. Stakeholders may hold different interests and agendas, some conflicting with others, and may demand both attention and resources. Therefore, managing conflict requires special skill sets, tools, and emphasis. This challenge requires strategic thinking, having a clear sense of values, and leveraging existing systems to make an informed choice.

The first step that a leader can take in managing conflicts is to **acknowledge different stakeholders and engage with them intimately.** Open and empathic communication is paramount during consultations to acknowledge the interest and achieve optimized returns that align all interests to organization-wide benefits. This step can help build a more considerate dialogue tree, link support networks, and identify what is needed to address stakeholders' demands and how each will support delivering tasks at the fore.

The second step is **goal alignment**. Leaders should ensure that the overall goals and vision of the organization are clear, communicated, and understood by all interest groups. When conflicting demands arise, leaders can reference these shared objectives to guide decision-making and resolve conflicts based on the broader strategic direction.

The third strategy is to **build an environment of cooperation and collaborative decision-making**. Encouraging collaboration among different interest groups can help manage conflicting demands. Leaders can convene cross-functional teams or committees that represent diverse perspectives and expertise, fostering a sense of collective ownership in decision-making processes.

Lastly, leaders should **prioritize conflicting demands**, considering the impact and urgency of each request. Some demands may need immediate attention; others may require longer-term strategies. Effectively prioritizing conflicting demands ensures that efforts are focused on those areas that contribute most to the organization's success. Prioritization should be accompanied by effective communication with all different interest groups.

INFINITE IMPACT

Political faces and superpowers

NAVIGATING CORPORATE POLITICS

Before we move on to the next topic, take a look at these political faces. Some are superpowers for getting things done. Some might be considered good, and others bad. I am leaving a bit of space under each picture to write the name of the person you think of when you read the description.

The **Know-it-all** is not only an expert in their field but takes excessive pride in their superior knowledge and expertise in the organization.

The **Puppet master** remains in the shadows, promoting the idea of leading from behind and often manipulating other key players within the organization to advance their personal agenda and influence decision-making.

The **Fixer** is a leader whose superpowers lie in resolving critical issues without disrupting the work and revitalizing stagnant and criticized projects.

The **Collaborator** champions diversity at work by inspiring teamwork, creating and developing communication frameworks, and creating blueprints for shared success.

The **Superhero** is a leader who has emerged out of universal respect and trust, selflessly and proactively helping people with business initiatives and personal problems and maintaining a culture of workplace positivity and triumph.

The **Networker** frequently chats with stakeholders and uses their networks to achieve professional objectives and outcomes.

The **Visionary** imposes inspirational visions and originality around colleagues and imprints optimally driven goals for projects.

The **Whisperer** possesses a special talent for seeding ideas into colleagues' minds to evoke good outcomes. The Whisperer is also a leader with the power to anonymously influence colleagues and create insidious agendas clandestinely.

The **Intimidator** uses bullying tactics to obtain what they demand and see results generated.

The **Survivor** demonstrates survivability by recovering alongside teams from organizational issues such as rejuvenation, legalities, and navigating market fluctuations.

The **Terminator** is tasked with the unfortunate role of shutting down failing company programs at a profile level.

The **Educationalist** is a leader who cultivates continuous learning for their workforce by investing in career development, promoting skills acquisition, and continuing education.

The **Profit Hunter** prioritizes and maximizes their focus on ROI (return on investment) for shareholders and exceeds sales goals.

The **Inclusivist** works toward employee inclusion, advocating for diversification initiatives.

The **Authoritarian** is a leader with unfair enabling who prioritizes personal interests and disregards teammates for personal gratification.

6

EMBRACING DIVERSITY, EQUITY, AND INCLUSION FOR A STRONGER FUTURE

Understanding the benefits of a diverse and inclusive workplace

If you are a leader in a multinational company, then you know that diversity, equity, and inclusion (DEI) is a priority on your agenda because it increases innovation, employee engagement, and retention. And if you are a leader in a company that does not prioritize it, I hope you will consider prioritizing it after reading this chapter.

By fostering an environment that embraces diversity in all its forms—whether it be gender, race, ethnicity, age, or background—you can unlock the vast potential of your workforce and create a vibrant atmosphere that nurtures creativity, collaboration, and excellence. Having a diverse team also comes with unique challenges that we all need to acknowledge. I will discuss most of them in this chapter.

First and foremost, a diverse and inclusive workplace cultivates a wide variety of perspectives, ideas, and experiences. We should all know this by now. Corporate leaders who prioritize diversity understand that different backgrounds and perspectives bring unique insights and approaches to problem-solving. By embracing this diversity, leaders can harness the collective intelligence of their team, enabling them to tackle challenges from multiple angles and arrive at more robust solutions.

Secondly, a diverse and inclusive workplace breeds innovation. Studies have shown that diverse teams are more likely to generate new ideas, challenge the status quo, and foster a culture that values creativity. A corporate leader who encourages diversity fosters an environment where employees feel empowered to share diverse opinions and unique viewpoints, sparking innovative thinking and transforming the organization's ability to adapt and succeed in rapidly evolving markets.

Moreover, a diverse and inclusive workplace enhances employee engagement and retention. When individuals feel valued and respected for who they are, they become more committed to their work and the organization as a whole. Corporate leaders who champion diversity and inclusion create an environment where employees can bring their whole selves to work, leading to increased job satisfaction, loyalty, and productivity.

Additionally, a diverse workforce enhances problem-solving capabilities and customer relationships. With a variety of backgrounds, talents, and perspectives, a diverse team can approach challenges from different angles. This diversity of thought enables leaders to make well-informed decisions, anticipate customer needs more accurately, and deepen relationships with diverse client bases by empathizing and understanding different perspectives.

By embracing diversity, leaders unlock the full potential of their teams, fuel innovation, enhance employee engagement, promote creativity, and deepen customer relationships. A diverse and inclusive workplace is not only morally right, but also vital for driving organizational success in an increasingly diverse and interconnected world.

The challenges of navigating DEI as a leader

Navigating diversity and inclusion as a leader comes with its own set of challenges, including unconscious bias and intergroup conflict. As leaders strive to create inclusive environments, it is important to address these challenges head-on, fostering awareness, empathy, and open communication to build bridges and promote collaboration.

Unconscious bias can pose a significant hurdle to leadership. Often rooted in societal stereotypes and ingrained assumptions, it can influence decision-making and impede the objective evaluation of talent and potential. Leaders should recognize and confront their own biases, develop self-awareness, and engage in ongoing education to mitigate their impact. By working hard to uncover and challenge unconscious biases, leaders can promote fair, inclusive practices that embrace diversity and foster equal opportunities for all. I believe that the starting point to dealing with unconscious bias is for each of us to admit that, whether we like it or not, we have our own biases.

Intergroup conflict is another challenge that leaders need to navigate in diverse workplaces. When individuals from different backgrounds and perspectives come together, clashes can arise due to differing experiences, values, and expectations. Leaders can tackle intergroup conflict by encouraging open dialogue, fostering a culture of respect and appreciation for diversity, and providing training on conflict resolution, effective communication, and crucial conversations. By creating an environment that values and celebrates differences while promoting understanding and collaboration, leaders can help bridge gaps and transcend intergroup conflict.

Embracing these challenges head-on is a testament to effective leadership and promotes a culture of inclusivity and collaboration within organizations.

Strategies for promoting DEI at all levels of the organization

Promoting diversity and inclusion in your team is crucial if you are a first-line manager. If you are a senior leader, you should do so at all levels. Here are some strategies that leaders can adopt to foster an environment that embraces diversity and fosters inclusion:

1. Establish realistic **DEI policies** everyone can follow: Develop and communicate clear policies that emphasize the organization's commitment to diversity and inclusion. These policies should outline expectations, provide guidelines for behavior, and promote fair and equitable practices, whether these relate to hiring, promoting, training and development, employee benefits, leave, or any other policy. Looking at market practice is also helpful, but bear in mind that sometimes market practices lag, which gives you an edge to become the leader of positive change.
2. Foster **inclusive leadership**: Leaders should serve as role models by demonstrating inclusive behaviors. Through inclusive leadership, they create an environment that encourages open dialogue, values diverse perspectives, and promotes a culture of respect and collaboration. Unfortunately, many leaders promote DEI on paper and lack the day-to-day actions to support the DEI strategy.
3. Implement **fair** and **inclusive hiring practices**: Review and revise recruitment and selection practices to ensure they are unbiased and promote diversity. Incorporate diverse interview panels, blind résumé screening, and diverse sourcing strategies to attract a broader range of qualified candidates. Some programs can assess the language of your job description and tell you if it is gender-neutral or

not. If DEI is not part of your talent acquisition team, consider adding it.

4. Provide **diversity** and **inclusion training**: Offer regular training programs to raise awareness about unconscious biases, cultural competence, and inclusive practices. This allows employees at all levels to challenge their own biases and acquire skills to foster inclusive interactions and decision-making.
5. Support **employee resource groups** (ERGs): Establish and support ERGs that bring together individuals with similar backgrounds or identities. These groups provide opportunities for networking, mentorship, and professional development, facilitating a sense of belonging and fostering inclusivity.
6. Create **inclusive communication channels**: Foster an open and inclusive communication environment by providing opportunities for all employees to express their ideas, concerns, and suggestions. Encourage open dialogue across all levels of the organization, ensuring that everyone's voice is heard and valued.
7. Make **diversity** and **inclusion part** of **performance evaluation**: Include diversity and inclusion as part of performance evaluation criteria. This sends a strong message that the organization values and rewards inclusive behaviors and contributions to diversity initiatives.
8. Establish **diversity metrics** and **accountability**: Set measurable goals and monitor progress toward diversity and inclusion targets. Hold leaders accountable for meeting these goals and regularly report and communicate progress to ensure transparency and commitment to

improvement. I would be very careful with using metrics and quotas because you do not want to end up adversely discriminating against other groups for the sake of achieving your quota.

Let's be frank. It is not going to be easy to create a diverse team. Not all talents are available in all groups. Most of the time, you have a tight hiring timeline, and your unconscious bias affects your decisions even if you do not want to admit it. And so many other reasons. But the one thing that I can guarantee is that if you believe that giving equal employment opportunities is the right thing to do and focus on talent instead of anything else, your team will bring more value than any nondiverse team will.

I supported DEI in an oil and gas company in 2012. We were trying to increase the gender-diversity ratios in technical roles in the Middle East—i.e., roles outside marketing, HR, legal, or administration. This means we wanted women in the Middle East to work on the rig site, in the middle of the desert, in the ocean, or pretty much anywhere. They were working on-call and then sent to the rig site, where they stayed for a month or more, living in a caravan in extreme conditions. Many employees, leaders, and even customers resisted it in the beginning. Staff of the rig site were all men. Most of these men were blue-collar and not ready to accept working with a female, let alone taking orders from a female engineer.

Interestingly, once we started looking, we found many excited, passionate, competent, and motivated females to do the job, no matter how hard it was. We just needed to start looking!

I admit the task was not easy. Despite introducing diversity policies and leadership and employee training, ensuring that the rig site was equipped with female-friendly facilities, promoting our plan to universities, sharing success stories, engaging with organizations supporting the cause, working on our culture readiness, and many other actions, we did not achieve great results overnight. We had to accept that it was a process. I always tell my colleagues in industries such as fast-moving consumer goods, technology, banking, etc. that if the oil and gas service industry was able to improve their DEI ratios, anyone could.

Examples of organizations that have successfully embraced DEI

- **Microsoft** has made diversity and inclusion a central focus within its organization. By implementing programs such as unconscious bias training and diverse hiring initiatives, it has worked toward creating a more inclusive workplace. This commitment to diversity has not only enhanced employee morale and engagement, but also brought about tangible business results. For instance, the company's diverse and inclusive culture has been linked to increased innovation and product development, allowing Microsoft to remain competitive in the tech industry.
- **Procter & Gamble (P&G)** has implemented inclusive talent practices and initiatives such as affinity groups and

diversity training programs. Such efforts have resulted in a more inclusive corporate culture, strengthening its ability to connect with diverse consumer markets. By developing products that cater to various communities and promoting an inclusive brand image, P&G has gained a competitive edge in capturing the loyalty of a diverse customer base.

- **Salesforce** is widely known for its commitment to diversity and inclusion. The company has not only implemented progressive policies, such as pay equity assessments and diverse candidate interview processes, but also actively used its platform to advocate for equality and inclusion. Salesforce accommodates employees from diverse backgrounds and has cultivated employee resource groups focused on various diversity dimensions. The organization's commitment to diversity and inclusion has improved its bottom line, with increased employee retention, improved customer satisfaction, and enhanced innovation.

- **Accenture**, a global consulting and professional services firm, has made significant strides in embracing diversity and inclusion. The company's strategy includes initiatives such as setting diversity goals, creating training programs, and implementing programs to recruit and retain diverse talent. Accenture's focus on diversity and inclusion has contributed to its success, resulting in improved innovation, increased productivity, and enhanced employee engagement. By cultivating an inclusive environment where unique perspectives are valued, Accenture has been able to better serve its clients and adapt to the changing needs of the marketplace.

The importance of ongoing measurement and evaluation of DEI efforts

Measuring and evaluating diversity and inclusion efforts is crucial for organizations to understand the impact of their strategies and initiatives. The importance of ongoing measurement lies in the ability to track progress, identify areas for improvement, and make data-driven decisions that promote a diverse and inclusive workplace.

Hard metrics, such as representation and retention rates, provide tangible evidence of an organization's commitment to diversity and inclusion. By monitoring these metrics, leaders can assess whether their efforts are leading to measurable changes in the composition of the workforce and identify any disparities or barriers that may exist. Tracking representation and retention allows organizations to set clear goals and objectives for increasing diversity and improving inclusion.

However, it is equally essential to consider the softer intangible aspects when evaluating diversity and inclusion efforts. Employee satisfaction and engagement are key indicators of the success of these initiatives. Organizations that prioritize diversity and inclusion not only create a more inclusive environment, but also enhance employee morale and motivation. When employees feel valued, heard, and included, they are more likely to be satisfied with their work and contribute to the organization's success.

Measuring and evaluating these softer intangibles can be done through employee surveys, focus groups, and regular feedback sessions. Such methods provide valuable insights into how employees perceive the organization's diversity and inclusion efforts, as well as identifying areas for improvement. By monitoring employee satisfaction and engagement, organizations can continuously assess the effectiveness of their strategies and adjust as needed to foster a more inclusive and supportive workplace.

7

MOTIVATION AND DRIVE

Understanding what motivation is and why it matters in the workplace

> *"Money motivates neither the best people nor the best in people. It can move the body and influence the mind, but it cannot touch the heart or move the spirit; that is reserved for belief, principle, and morality."*
>
> — Dee Hock
> Founder, Visa

Motivation is also one of the topics that has been discussed for decades. Without motivation, it would be challenging for you as a leader to drive results and creativity and push the organization's bottom line to its full potential. Highly respected practitioners and theorists talk about intrinsic versus extrinsic motivation, and there are many traditional motivational theories, starting with Maslow's Hierarchy of Needs. I will only touch on a selection of the most notable ones and suggest you do further readings on them (and others) if they interest you.

1. **Maslow's Hierarchy of Needs**: This theory proposed by Abraham Maslow suggests that individuals have a hierarchy of needs, ranging from physiological needs (food and shelter) to self-actualization needs (personal growth and fulfillment). According to Maslow, individuals are motivated to fulfill lower-level needs before moving on to higher-level needs.
2. **Alderfer's ERG Theory**: Clayton Alderfer's theory builds on Maslow's Hierarchy of Needs, stating that we have three core needs: existence, relatedness, and growth.
3. **Herzberg's Two-Factor Theory** (also known as Motivation–Hygiene Theory or Dual-Factor Theory): Developed by Frederick Herzberg, this theory distinguishes between motivators (challenging work) and hygiene factors (salary, work conditions) that influence job satisfaction and motivation. According to Herzberg, motivators lead to satisfaction, and hygiene factors prevent dissatisfaction.
4. **Adams' Equity Theory**: Developed by J. Stacy Adams, the equity theory states that individuals compare their inputs (effort, skills) and outcomes (rewards, recognition) to those of others. If they perceive an inequity, either in

underpayment or overpayment, relative to others, it affects their motivation and satisfaction.

5. **Vroom's Expectancy Theory**: Victor Vroom's expectancy theory suggests that motivation depends on three factors: expectancy (the belief that effort leads to performance), instrumentality (the belief that performance leads to desired outcomes), and valence (the value individuals place on the expected outcomes). According to this theory, individuals are motivated when they expect their efforts to result in desired outcomes.
6. **Deci and Ryan's Self-determination Theory**: Developed by Edward L. Deci and Richard M. Ryan, self-determination theory focuses on intrinsic motivation, autonomy, and the fulfillment of psychological needs. It suggests that individuals are motivated when their inherent psychological needs for autonomy, competence, and relatedness are satisfied.
7. **Locke's Goal-setting Theory**: Pioneered by Edwin Locke, the goal-setting theory states that setting specific and challenging goals enhances motivation and performance. This theory emphasizes the importance of clarity, commitment, and feedback to improve effectiveness.
8. **Skinner's Reinforcement Theory**: B. F. Skinner's reinforcement theory suggests that behavior is influenced by reinforcement and punishment. It focuses on the consequences of actions and how they shape behavior. Positive reinforcement aims to increase desired behaviors, while negative reinforcement seeks to reduce or eliminate undesired behaviors.

9. **Deci's Cognitive Evaluation Theory**: Proposed by Edward L. Deci, the cognitive evaluation theory explains how extrinsic rewards can either enhance or undermine intrinsic motivation. It suggests that factors such as autonomy, competence, and relatedness can influence the impact of extrinsic rewards on intrinsic motivation.
10. **Bandura's Self-Efficacy Theory**: Developed by Albert Bandura, self-efficacy theory explains how individuals' beliefs in their ability to perform tasks affect motivation. According to this theory, individuals with high self-efficacy are more likely to set ambitious goals, exert effort, and persist in the face of challenges.
11. **McClelland's Achievement Motivation Theory** (also known as Theory of Needs): This theory, developed by David McClelland, focuses on the need for achievement, affiliation, and power. It suggests that individuals are motivated when they have a strong need for achievement and strive for excellence to meet self-defined goals.
12. **Festinger's Cognitive Dissonance Theory**: Proposed by Leon Festinger, cognitive dissonance theory suggests that individuals are motivated to reduce the discomfort (dissonance) between their beliefs, attitudes, and actions. When there is inconsistency, individuals are motivated to change their attitudes or behaviors.

There are many more motivational theories out there. It isn't easy to memorize and understand all of them, nor is it easy to refer to them in each situation, especially since your organization might also have other tools and processes for motivation, reward, and recognition. But it is up to you as a leader to familiarize yourself with at least some of them.

Back to basics

Organizations tend to invest in many tools, fancy terms, and sophisticated systems with long charts and guidelines and push them on leaders with the effect of confusing rather than guiding them. If you can utilize your internal tools, that's fantastic. However, don't skip the basics.

Know them

When leaders brag about everything they learned in their master's degree or Ph.D. and start using all the fancy terms about business and leadership, and yet their team is underperforming, demotivated, with high turnover, and no one wants to work with them, you know something is missing. What's missing are the fundamentals of human relationships—the simple conversations you have with your direct reports that allow you to understand how they are feeling and give insight into how each reacts to different stimuli. Most people are not motivated by the same tools, and no book on this planet will help you motivate them unless you first get to know them better. Therefore, try as much as you can to spend more time with them. Once you do that, you will realize you are better positioned to motivate them.

Listen to them

Money is essential to achieve basic needs—we all agree we need to get paid. Money will always be a significant reward, but I believe it will only work long-term for specific people and jobs. Once paid competitively, other factors will be more telling.

A woman named Diana, relatively new to the organization, was astonished at the level of motivation in the team spread across the globe. She could not tell why these people were so highly motivated, even though they worked thousands of miles from each other. What could be the one thing leaders were doing right that all of them would give their sweat and tears to this company? Diana noted that at the end of a staff meeting, the global Vice President said, "I do not care how you get things done. I trust that you will do the best for the company and the people within the organization, and I will support you every step of the way." That was it. She realized that the one thing that all leaders were doing was mirroring their VP, creating a culture of empowerment, autonomy, and trust. Because this company trusted its people, its leaders gave them the space and ability to do what they thought was right, making their people more responsible, loyal, and creative.

Autonomy is one of the key motivators. If you believe that you hired the right people, let them tell you how they can do their jobs better; this is why you hired them. You did not hire them to tell them exactly what needs to be done. You hired them because you thought they could add value to your business, which is where the best ideas come from. Autonomy can sometimes be precarious if you are working in a place where structure, processes, and standards are crucial, such as an oil rig. If one thing goes wrong, you could cause a non-productive time, huge losses, or a blowout. Literally, you could blow the well out! As a leader, you need to know when it is beneficial to let your employees work on their tasks the way they think would generate the best results, knowing that you are all aligned with the common goal.

Identify them

The easiest people to motivate are those who are self-motivated. In my interviews, many managers ask me why I focus a lot on motivational fit and if it is not enough to focus on the job experience and the right behaviors. I do agree that job experience and behavioral competencies are crucial. Still, I also believe that if you hire a person whose values are aligned with the company values and you have a shared purpose, this person will do so much better than someone who is only qualified in terms of job experience. If you are in a leadership position, hire those who have a similar purpose to the one you and your corporation have. They will come energized every day and make remarkable achievements. When I asked Manish Gordhan, Global VP of SAP based in London, what he looked for when he hired people in his team, disregarding the roles and responsibilities, he answered, "I look for drive and enthusiasm in the candidates."

Develop them

> *"Before you are a leader, success is all about growing yourself. When you become a leader, success is all about growing others."*
>
> —Jack Welch,
> Former CEO, General Electric

One of the other powerful motivational tools is progress and learning. Many leaders create a learning organization to ensure information and knowledge are disseminated to the team through different tools. Ronald Rejimers, VP of Adidas in the Netherlands, said, "My job is not to tell you what to do; my job is to help you further develop so you can kick me out of my chair."

Other leaders keep the knowledge to themselves. They think they can keep an edge this way and become irreplaceable to the organization. Some team members do the same. Unfortunately, these people will not achieve much by themselves; instead, they limit themselves, not knowing their true potential as leaders and even individual contributors. Progress could be in the form of knowledge, training, exposure, mentoring (lateral or upward, and sometimes a step backward) to learn something you might have missed along the way or help you move away from a stagnant place you may have reached. Your job as a leader is not only to identify your own strengths but also the strengths of your followers and position them where they fit the best.

Extrinsic vs. intrinsic

Understanding the differences between intrinsic and extrinsic motivation is crucial for leaders to motivate their teams and maximize productivity. Intrinsic motivation refers to the internal drive and enjoyment one derives from the task itself. It arises from personal interest, satisfaction, and a sense of fulfillment. On the other hand, extrinsic motivation comes from external factors such as the rewards, recognition, and incentives provided by others. Both intrinsic and extrinsic motivation have their merits.

Intrinsic motivation is often considered more powerful and long-lasting. When individuals are intrinsically motivated, they engage in their work for the joy and personal fulfillment it brings, leading to increased creativity, innovation, and job satisfaction. Intrinsic motivation taps into employees' passions and allows them to take ownership of their work, leading to higher-quality outcomes. It fosters a sense of autonomy, mastery, and purpose, which leads to sustained engagement and commitment.

Extrinsic motivation, while not as strong as intrinsic motivation, can still be effective in certain situations. External rewards and recognition, such as promotions or bonuses, can provide a sense of achievement and motivate individuals to perform tasks they might not be naturally inclined toward. Rewards tied to performance also provide clear goals and benchmarks for employees to strive for, increasing their focus and effort. Extrinsic motivation can be a valuable tool for short-term boosts in productivity or for tasks that might not inherently be interesting to individuals.

In reality, the most effective approach lies in finding a balance between intrinsic and extrinsic motivation strategies. By cultivating an environment that supports intrinsic motivation through factors like meaningful work, clear communication, and opportunities for development, leaders can tap into employees' internal drive while also providing appropriate rewards and recognition to reinforce desired behaviors. Understanding the individual needs and preferences of team members is key to tailoring an effective motivation strategy that combines intrinsic and extrinsic elements.

Roadblocks to employee motivation and engagement

Leaders should be aware of the potential roadblocks that can hinder employee motivation. Recognizing and addressing these roadblocks is vital for creating a positive and productive work environment. Here are some main roadblocks that you need to be aware of:

1. **Lack of clear goals and expectations**: When employees are unsure about their goals and what is expected of them, motivation can suffer. Leaders need to set clear and achievable goals, provide regular feedback, and ensure that employees understand their roles and responsibilities.

Clarity and transparency in communication are critical to keeping employees motivated and aligned with organizational objectives.
2. **Inadequate recognition and reward**s: Employees need to feel appreciated for their efforts and achievements. The absence of recognition and rewards can lead to demotivation. Effective leaders should establish a culture of recognition, openly acknowledging and appreciating employees' contributions, whether through verbal recognition, promotions, bonuses, or other incentives. Regular recognition programs help reinforce positive behaviors, boosting motivation and job satisfaction.
3. **Limited growth and development opportunitie**s: When employees don't see opportunities for growth, they may lose motivation. Leaders should prioritize employee development by offering training, mentorship programs, and career advancement opportunities. Providing avenues for skill-building and personal growth creates a sense of purpose, allowing employees to see a clear path to advancement within the organization.
4. **Lack of autonomy and** empowerment: Micromanagement and a lack of trust can limit employees' motivation. Leaders should foster a culture of autonomy and empowerment, giving employees the freedom to make decisions, take ownership of their work, and explore innovative ideas. Empowering employees shows trust and confidence in their abilities, increasing their motivation, creativity, and engagement.

5. **Poor work–life balance**: When employees experience constant pressure, excessive workload, or an imbalance between work and personal life, their motivation can suffer. Effective leaders prioritize work–life balance, promoting policies that support flexible schedules, vacation time, and stress management. Encouraging open dialogue about workloads, providing support for burnout prevention, and nurturing a healthy work environment can help maintain employee motivation and well-being.

8

FOSTERING PSYCHOLOGICAL SAFETY FOR TEAM EXCELLENCE

Psychological safety is the shared belief among team members that they can take risks and express themselves without fear of negative consequences. Psychological safety is an essential aspect of the workplace culture because it leads to better communication, more creativity, and higher levels of engagement, which ultimately leads to higher productivity and better outcomes for the organization. The concept of psychological safety was introduced and extensively studied by Harvard Business School Professor Amy Edmondson in her seminal work entitled "Psychological Safety and Learning Behavior in Work Teams."

The importance of psychological safety in the workplace is emphasized by the fact that it supports the ability of team members to speak up, share ideas, and collaborate on projects in a structured and supportive environment. The existence of psychological safety frees workers to engage in constructive disagreement and fosters an environment of respectful discourse that leads to better decision-making among team members. In practice, this means that employees are more likely to provide feedback and criticism without fear of retaliation or punishment, which leads to more productive and engaged teams.

Psychological safety is a non-traditional concept, but it is critical to the success of a modern-day workplace. Psychological safety leads to employees who feel empowered, more productive, and collaborative. The *Harvard Business Review* suggests implementing active listening and even designating time during meetings for casual conversations to foster psychological safety.

Identifying what contributes to the lack of psychological safety

Leadership plays a key role in cultivating an environment that fosters psychological safety. To achieve this, leaders should identify and address the factors contributing to a lack of psychological safety in their organization. A lack of clear communication or guidelines relating to behavior, for instance, can send mixed messages to employees and make them feel anxious or uncertain. Addressing this can involve investing in comprehensive communication strategies relating to open dialogue and feedback that leave no room for ambiguity.

Additionally, some organizational cultures discourage vulnerability, creativity, or risk-taking, leading to a lack of psychological safety. Leaders should identify such impediments to psychological safety in their organization and introduce measures that encourage these qualities in the workplace. This will help create a culture in which team members can take calculated risks and learn from the outcomes without feeling punished. Attention to these dimensions of psychological safety promoted by *Harvard Business Review*'s "The Fearless Organization: Creating Psychological Safety" is one possible approach, but it's up to each leader to determine how best to address these dynamics in their organization.

To cultivate psychological safety in the workplace, leaders should also address the barriers to effective decision-making. For instance, if individuals are unable to challenge decisions without fear of judgment, it can engender hostility and defensiveness, ultimately making the workplace a more tense and stressful environment. Instead, leaders need to encourage open dissent, not as an attack, but rather as a sign of active engagement by the employee. This strategy can help nurture innovation, establish more effective communication channels, and strengthen employee engagement. Promoting an active inclusion culture, listening intently to even minority reports, and seeking to be understanding and supportive of every employee's contribution can all help.

Tactical strategies for increasing psychological safety and security

Effective communication is vital to building a work culture based on inclusivity, accountability, and psychological safety. Here are some tactical strategies that leaders can use to promote openness, inclusivity, equity, and accountability in the workplace.

First, leaders can **facilitate an information-sharing culture** that supports everyone's participation. This culture is anchored in the recognition that each employee's contributions matter. The practice of informal and formal check-ins helps clarify where company goals are headed, and this can lead to creative and meaningful contributions that benefit everyone.

Second, as language is a critical component of creating psychological safety, leaders need to **be intentional about how they communicate** to ensure clarity of information and assuage confusion. They should also be sensitive to and careful not to reinforce bias in language usage. Making use of inclusive language that avoids gender biases, racial slurs, or discriminatory language that negatively stereotypes or tokenizes a particular group sets a decent tone for establishing an accountable, safe, and inclusive environment.

Third, leaders should **promote an open-door policy** where every employee feels valued, respected, and understood. When staff members feel listened to and heard, they are more likely to share their experiences, insights, and even innovative ideas, thus creating a healthy context for effective communication leading to a psychologically safe work culture.

Lastly, leaders should **use objective measures** to identify successes, areas in need of improvement, and comparisons of results for the evaluation of policies. When members of a team understand that their activity levels and accountability are measured objectively, it deepens their commitment to the goals and enhances their understanding that their participation and hard work contribute to achieving and quantifying their success.

9

LEADING A MULTI-GENERATIONAL WORKFORCE

Understanding generational diversity

Leaders need to understand the generational diversity in the employment market today and the potential tension points it may produce.

Step into most workplaces today and you will find a diverse array of generations without being able to identify their seniority levels, expertise, or influence. The fifty-year-old could be managing the thirty-year-old or vice versa. It has been portrayed perfectly by Robert De Niro and Anne Hathaway in their movie *The Intern*.

Each of these generations has its own unique set of values, professional aspirations, and work styles. Understanding these generational differences is increasingly crucial for leaders to promote unity, collaboration, and a productive work environment, while also avoiding potential tension points in the workplace.

Generally, leadership techniques that fit one generation might not be as effective for another generation. Thus, a flexible approach needs to be taken. It is important to know the potential tension points between generational cohorts to help prevent intergenerational misunderstandings. Effective communication should be used to address these differences and help bridge any gaps. Establishing formal and informal channels of communication can foster better collaboration and increase generational understanding, encouraging participation and active involvement in joint projects among different generations and incentivizing cross-generational mentorship.

Inspiration, empathy, and motivation provide a framework for cultures of inclusivity in the workplace. Therefore, leaders need to embrace an approach that reflects these ideas about the different generations. Maintaining an open, transparent culture by listening with empathy to concerns and views conveyed by members of other generations can enhance teamwork and moral satisfaction significantly.

Understanding generational diversity within the employment market remains critical in fostering a work environment that values the experience and knowledge of all generations, welcomes unique styles of work, and promotes continuous learning, creativity, and innovation from all persons. Leaders who attend to both the perks and potential barriers and conflicts of generational diversity successfully in their work environments will create a harmonious and prosperous workplace.

Understanding the common stereotypes and pitfalls of generational diversity

There are currently four to five generations in the workforce, depending on how the generations are divided. Here, you will see a brief description of each one and the most common stereotypes attached to each. Remember, these are only stereotypes.

1. **Traditionalists or the Silent Generation**: This generation refers to those who were born before 1946. They are known to be hardworking, risk-averse, disciplined, and loyal to their employers. Stereotypes include that they do not adapt well to change and may not be as receptive to technological changes as younger generations.

2. **Baby Boomers**: Individuals born between 1946 and 1964 belong to this generation. Boomers led the post-World War II

population boom and represented a large generation in the modern workforce. Boomers are credited with bringing notions of personal freedom and individualism to the workforce. They are known to be independent, hardworking, and ambitious. Stereotypes suggest they may be stubborn or resistant to change and technologically challenged—i.e., they may not embrace modern technology easily.

3. **Generation X**: Individuals born between 1965 and 1980 make up this generation. Xers are known to be independent, self-reliant, and entrepreneurial. Stereotypes of Xers indicate they are resourceful, independent thinkers and goal-driven leaders. Xers prefer to keep work and home life separate and place a high value on work–life balance.

4. **Millennial or Gen Y**: The millennials were born between 1981 and 1996. They are identified with the introduction of new technology and communication methods that include social

media. They have a reputation for being idealistic and optimistic yet have little tolerance for bureaucracy and traditional hierarchies. Older generations tend to eye them cynically, disregarding their interest in personal growth and their passionate dedication to their workspaces.

5. Gen Z: Those born between 1997 and the 2010s compose the current generation. They are digital natives known for their technological aptitude and creativity. According to Handshake's 2020 "From Hey to Hired" report, survey participants attributed to Gen Zers skills such as adaptability, problem-solving, and good communication skills.

Notably, these are generalizations or assumptions, and they do not represent the full picture of each generational group. Individuals may vary in their personalities, technical abilities, and approaches to work regardless of the era in which they were born.

Challenges and benefits of having a multigenerational workforce

The modern workforce is composed of people of different generations, and paying attention to each generation's unique characteristics may help improve communication, management, and performance. However, understanding generational diversity can be challenging, constantly in flux, and prone to different interpretations. Overall, generational differences have the potential to be both a challenge and an opportunity.

Let's start with the potential challenges.

1. **Communication styles**: Different generations have distinct communication preferences, which can lead to misunderstandings and a lack of effective collaboration. For instance, older employees may prefer face-to-face communication, while younger ones may rely more on technology-mediated communication like email or instant messaging.
2. **Technological fluency**: Bridging the digital divide can be a challenge, particularly for older employees who may struggle with new technologies. This can limit their ability to work efficiently and hinder their collaboration with tech-savvy younger colleagues. For instance, an older employee may have difficulty using a new project management software, affecting their productivity and ability to communicate effectively with the rest of the team.

3. **Work–life balance**: Younger generations often prioritize work–life balance, seeking flexible work arrangements and emphasizing personal interests and well-being. This can clash with the work habits of older generations, who are more accustomed to longer work hours and have a stronger dedication to work. For example, a younger employee requesting to work remotely to maintain a healthier work–life balance may be seen as "slacking off" by an older colleague who values face-to-face interaction and a traditional work schedule.
4. **Leadership styles**: Each generation tends to value different leadership styles due to differing expectations and experiences. For example, younger generations often expect more collaborative and participatory leadership styles that foster openness and innovation. In contrast, older generations may be more familiar with hierarchical leadership structures, where decision-making authority rests with a few senior individuals.
5. **Knowledge transfer**: Capturing and sharing knowledge across generations can be challenging, especially with older employees nearing retirement. As they possess valuable institutional knowledge, organizations need to ensure effective knowledge transfer to younger employees. For instance, a senior employee with extensive technical expertise may be the only one aware of certain company-specific processes or historical information, creating a knowledge gap if this information is not adequately transferred.

6. **Skill development**: Different generations may have varied learning preferences and needs, requiring tailored approaches to skill development. For example, older employees might benefit from more traditional classroom-type training, while younger employees might prefer gamified or interactive online learning platforms.
7. **Perception and stereotypes**: Overcoming stereotypes and negative perceptions can be an obstacle to effective collaboration across generational lines. For instance, older employees may perceive younger employees as entitled or overly reliant on technology, while younger employees may perceive older employees as resistant to change or technologically inept. These stereotypes can hinder productivity.
8. **Career advancement**: Providing equal opportunities for career advancement and growth across generations can be challenging. Organizations should strike a balance between honoring experience and tenure while also providing opportunities for younger talent to grow and contribute. For example, a younger employee may feel frustrated if a promotion is given to a more experienced colleague solely based on tenure without considering their own skills and potential.
9. **Work ethic**: Diverse work ethics and expectations, such as workplace flexibility and attention to task completion, can create friction in a multigenerational workforce. For instance, younger employees who value flexibility and work–life integration might clash with older employees who prioritize dedication to the job and strict adherence to traditional work hours.

LEADING A MULTI-GENERATIONAL WORKFORCE

You may wonder why companies still try to push for a multigenerational workforce with all the challenges it represents. First of all, most of these challenges could be solved by having clear communication, equal employment opportunities, transparency, empathy, and strong policies. Here are some potential opportunities:

1. **Diversity of skills and perspectives**: With each generation bringing unique skills, experiences, and perspectives to the table, a multigenerational workforce can offer a rich pool of knowledge and expertise. For example, older employees may have years of industry experience and institutional knowledge that younger employees can learn from, while younger workers may bring fresh ideas and technological proficiency to the team.
2. **Enhanced collaboration and innovation**: By leveraging the diverse skills and perspectives of different generations, organizations can foster a more collaborative and innovative work environment. For instance, a group that includes both experienced employees and younger talent can benefit from a blend of creativity, critical thinking, and practical expertise when working together on complex projects or problem-solving initiatives.
3. **Mentoring and knowledge transfer**: Multigenerational teams provide opportunities for formal and informal mentoring, helping to transfer valuable knowledge from experienced employees to younger ones. For example, older employees can mentor younger team members, enabling them to develop skills and learn from past experiences.

4. **Continuous learning and skill development**: Different generations in the workforce can inspire and challenge each other to continue learning and developing new skills. For instance, younger employees can share their knowledge of the latest technologies and trends with older colleagues, while older employees can offer guidance on building relationships and navigating professional challenges based on their experience.
5. **Flexibility and adaptability**: A multigenerational workforce can be more adaptable to change and addressing challenges, as employees from different generations often have varying levels of comfort with change. When handled well, this diversity in attitude toward change can be leveraged to adapt to evolving market conditions and business needs.
6. **Enhanced customer understanding and engagement**: With a diverse range of ages and backgrounds, a multigenerational workforce can provide valuable insights into different customer segments. For example, younger employees can offer insights into the preferences and behaviors of younger customer demographics, while older employees may bring insights into the needs of older customers.
7. **Stronger succession planning**: Having a multigenerational workforce can contribute to better succession planning, ensuring smooth transitions and knowledge continuity within the organization. For example, organizations can identify high-potential younger employees and provide opportunities for their development, preparing them to step into key roles when older employees retire.

8. **Increased employee engagement and retention**: Offering a multigenerational workforce can promote employee engagement and retention, as it demonstrates an inclusive and supportive work environment that values and incorporates diverse perspectives. This can contribute to higher job satisfaction and loyalty. For example, younger employees may be attracted to organizations that offer mentorship programs or opportunities for cross-generational collaboration.
9. **Innovative problem solving**: Different generations often bring different problem-solving approaches, which can lead to more creative and effective solutions. For example, a team working on a complex challenge may benefit from the combination of analytical and research skills from older employees, coupled with fresh insights and out-of-the-box thinking from younger team members.
10. **Organizational learning and adaptability**: A multigenerational workforce promotes organizational learning and adaptability by continuously exposing the organization to new ideas, perspectives, and skills. For example, an organization that encourages cross-generational knowledge sharing and collaboration creates an environment that quickly adapts to changing markets and embraces innovation.

10

OVERCOMING BURNOUT AND PRIORITIZING WELLNESS

Recognizing burnout as a real and prevalent issue in the modern workplace is of utmost importance for leaders and organizations. Burnout refers to a state of chronic physical and emotional exhaustion resulting from prolonged stress and excessive work demands. With the rise in remote work and the blurred boundaries between work and personal life, burnout has become even more prevalent. It harms individuals' mental health, overall well-being, and their ability to perform at their best. Acknowledging burnout as a legitimate concern is the first step toward addressing and mitigating its effects.

Numerous studies have highlighted the prevalence and impact of burnout in the workplace. Research by Maslach and Leiter (1997) established the Maslach Burnout Inventory (MBI), a widely recognized tool for measuring burnout levels. The World Health Organization now recognizes burnout as an occupational phenomenon contributing to physical and mental health issues. A study by Mullen et al. (2019) found that burnout is negatively associated with job satisfaction and positively associated with turnover intentions. These findings highlight the need for leaders to understand and address burnout in their teams.

Leaders can play a pivotal role in preventing and managing burnout by cultivating a culture that promotes work–life balance, emphasizes self-care, and supports the well-being of their team members. This includes encouraging breaks and time off, setting realistic expectations, and actively listening to employee concerns. Offering coaching and mentoring support, fostering a positive work environment, and providing resources for stress management can significantly mitigate burnout risk.

Furthermore, organizations should invest in employee well-being initiatives and provide resources for skill-building resilience and stress reduction. Offering flexible work arrangements, promoting effective workload management strategies, and fostering a supportive and inclusive culture can go a long way to addressing burnout. Taking a proactive approach to preventing and managing burnout not only benefits individuals, but also contributes to overall employee engagement, productivity, and organizational success.

In the last four years, I have been hearing about burnout and mental health cases more than ever. One of the good outcomes of COVID-19 is that people came to recognize their health as a priority. Organizations have recognized that if they don't support employees' well-being, they will not be attractive or competitive, which was one of the reasons for the "great resignation" during the pandemic. Unfortunately, not all industries and companies implement these strategies, but I believe everyone will have to catch up eventually.

Causes and symptoms of burnout

Understanding the causes and symptoms of burnout, such as chronic stress, excessive workload, and a feeling of detachment, is crucial for leaders to recognize and address this issue within their teams effectively. Burnout can stem from a multitude of factors that contribute to chronic stress and exhaustion.

Let's look at some of the main causes and symptoms of burnout so you can avoid them as a leader (as much as possible):

1. **Workload overload**: An overwhelming amount of work and unforgiving deadlines.
2. **Lack of job control**: Limited autonomy and decision-making power can make employees feel trapped and disempowered.
3. **Poor work–life balance**: Extensive work hours encroaching on one's private life and the inability to disconnect from work.
4. **Unrealistic expectations**: Unrealistic demands and pressure for perfection can result in excessive stress and exhaustion.

5. **Lack of recognition**: Feeling undervalued and underappreciated can erode motivation and contribute to burnout.
6. **Insufficient resources**: Inadequate resources, such as time, tools, or support, can hinder productivity and increase stress levels.
7. **Lack of social support**: Isolation and minimal social interaction within the workplace can sap motivation.
8. **Role ambiguity**: Unclear job expectations and responsibilities can create confusion and anxiety, leading to burnout.
9. **Organizational culture**: Toxic workplaces with a culture of hostility, bad politics, or poor leadership.
10. **Lack of growth opportunities**: Limited opportunities for skill development and career advancement can lead to stagnation and burnout.
11. **Poor communication**: Ineffective communication channels and lack of open dialogue can cause frustration and stress over time.
12. **Mismatched values**: These occur when personal values are not aligned with those of the organization.
13. **Emotional demands**: Dealing with emotionally challenging situations or difficult clients can take a toll on mental well-being.
14. **Unclear expectations**: Uncertainty around goals, performance measures, or feedback can generate anxiety.

Leaders need to be vigilant of these causes and recognize the symptoms of burnout in their team members, such as chronic fatigue, decreased motivation, increased cynicism, and decreased productivity. By addressing the underlying causes and implementing strategies to mitigate burnout, leaders can promote a healthy and high-performing work environment.

Strategies to balance workload and eliminate stress

Part of a leader's role is to implement strategies to balance workload and eliminate aspects of the work environment that are causing stress for employees.

Improving well-being and avoiding burnout is going to be one of your essential tasks if you want to keep leading a sustainable team, improve productivity, and manage the attrition rate—and sometimes employee escalations to unions and work councils. Here are ten suggested strategies that corporate leaders can implement to promote well-being and prevent burnout:

1. **Start prioritizing it yourself**: You, as a leader, need to prioritize your own self-care to maintain your physical and mental health. This can include engaging in regular exercise, practicing mindfulness or meditation, getting enough sleep, and maintaining a healthy work–life balance.
2. **Delegate effectively**: Delegate tasks and responsibilities to your team members, enabling them to develop their skills and take on additional responsibilities. Effective delegation not only reduces the workload but also empowers team members and fosters their growth.

3. **Set boundaries**: Establish clear boundaries between work and personal life. Setting specific work hours, avoiding excessive overtime, and taking regular breaks allow leaders to recharge and avoid burnout.
4. **Foster a positive work environment**: A positive work environment is crucial for employee well-being and engagement. Encourage a culture of open communication, collaboration, and mutual support that recognizes and celebrates achievements, provides constructive feedback, and promotes work–life integration. All these factors contribute to a healthy and supportive workplace.
5. **Encourage well-being programs**: Initiate and support well-being programs. This can include offering employee assistance programs, providing resources for stress management or mental health support, and promoting initiatives related to physical fitness and nutrition.
6. **Maintain a supportive network**: Prioritize building and nurturing a strong support network, both within and outside the organization. This can involve seeking guidance or mentorship from other leaders, participating in professional networks, or joining peer support groups.
7. **Create opportunities for growth**: Provide opportunities for professional development and growth to prevent burnout. Leaders can support their team members by offering training programs, coaching, and mentoring, allowing for both personal and career growth.
8. **Promote flexibility**: Offer flexible work arrangements such as remote work, flextime, or compressed work weeks. These will enhance well-being and work–life balance.

Leaders can champion these initiatives and establish policies that support flexibility within the organization.

9. **Foster emotional intelligence**: Develop emotional intelligence skills to better understand and manage your own emotions, as well as empathize with and support your team members. This will enhance communication, build strong relationships, and foster a positive work environment.
10. **Lead by example**: Perhaps the most impactful strategy is for corporate leaders to lead by example. Demonstrating healthy work habits, work–life balance, and practicing self-care serves as a model for others and inspires a positive well-being culture within the organization.
11. **Regularly monitor wellness metrics**: Metrics such as mental health rates and employee satisfaction scores can help you identify potential risk factors to improve and maintain associated business objectives.

Regularly monitoring wellness metrics is a proactive approach that leaders can adopt to ensure the well-being of their employees and achieve associated business objectives. Here are some techniques for you to consider using to monitor wellness metrics effectively:

1. **Establish metrics and benchmarks**: Identify relevant wellness metrics aligned with your business objectives. These can include mental health rates, employee satisfaction scores, absenteeism rates, or productivity indicators. Establishing baseline benchmarks will allow you to track progress and identify potential risk factors.

2. **Conduct regular surveys and assessments**: Implement regular surveys or assessments to gather valuable insights into the well-being of your employees. These surveys can focus on areas such as work–life balance, stress levels, job satisfaction, and overall engagement. Collecting feedback and data from employees will allow you to identify potential issues and take targeted action.
3. **Encourage open communication and feedback**: Encourage employees to provide feedback on their well-being, work-related challenges, and suggestions for improvement. This can be done through regular check-ins, confidential feedback mechanisms, or focus group discussions.
4. **Analyze and interpret data**: Once data are collected, analyze and interpret the metrics to identify patterns, trends, and potential risks. Using data visualization tools or working with data analysts can help you gain insights to inform decision-making and prioritize areas of focus for employee well-being improvement.
5. **Take proactive action**: Armed with the insights gained from wellness metrics, take proactive action to address potential risks and improve associated business objectives. This can involve implementing wellness programs, offering resources for stress management, addressing underlying organizational issues, or providing training and support for managers to promote a healthy work environment.

By regularly monitoring wellness metrics, analyzing data, and taking proactive action, corporate leaders can create a culture that prioritizes employee well-being, leading to improved engagement, productivity, and overall business success.

11

MASTERING REMOTE LEADERSHIP WITH IMPACT AND EMPATHY

In today's ever-evolving business environment, understanding the significance of remote leadership is crucial for success. If your competitors and the market are adopting remote working, you might have no option but to follow suit. Remote working could be very beneficial with the right leadership approach. Here are some benefits:

Firstly, remote leadership allows organizations **to tap into a global talent pool**. By embracing remote work, businesses can access an expansive talent pool from around the world, breaking down geographical barriers and diversifying their workforce. Remote leaders appreciate the power of building virtual relationships through leveraging communication technologies that foster collaboration, innovation, and a sense of unity among remote teams.

Secondly, remote leadership **promotes flexibility and work–life balance**. In this fast-paced, interconnected world, employees seek greater flexibility and the ability to find a balance between their personal and professional lives. Remote leaders understand the importance of trust, granting their teams the freedom and autonomy to manage their own schedules while maintaining high levels of productivity. With remote work, individuals can create work environments that align with their needs and work–life integration, resulting in increased job satisfaction, engagement, and overall well-being.

Thirdly, remote leadership **encourages resilience and adaptability**. Embracing remote work practices allows organizations to weather unexpected challenges. Whether they be natural disasters or unforeseen global crises, remote teams can seamlessly continue operations. Remote leaders harness the power of technology to foster effective communication, collaboration, and decision-making, ensuring agility and the ability to respond swiftly to changing circumstances.

Lastly, remote leadership **drives cost-effectiveness and sustainability**. Remote work reduces the need for physical office spaces, saving costs on rent, utilities, and maintenance. Beyond financial benefits, remote work contributes to sustainability efforts, reducing the carbon emissions associated with commuting. Remote leaders inspire their teams to work efficiently, leverage digital tools, and embrace remote operations, allowing organizations to make a positive environmental impact.

How to manage it effectively

Successfully managing remote teams requires a combination of effective leadership techniques and appropriate tools and strategies. Here are five ways to manage remote teams successfully:

1. **Establish clear communication channels**: Using tools like video conferencing, instant messaging, and project management platforms helps foster seamless communication and collaboration. Regular team meetings, one-on-one check-ins, and dedicated communication time foster transparency, ensure alignment, and create a sense of connection within remote teams.
2. **Set goals and manage performance**: Clearly defining goals and expectations is crucial for remote team success. Setting measurable objectives and KPIs provides a clear roadmap for everyone's work. Regularly tracking progress, providing feedback, and recognizing achievements help remote team members stay motivated and accountable.
3. **Build trustful relationships**: Trust forms the foundation for productive remote teams. Leaders should take intentional steps to build trust among team members who may be geographically dispersed. Regular virtual team-building activities, creating opportunities for social interaction, and encouraging open and honest communication help to foster strong relationships and camaraderie.
4. **Foster flexibility and work–life balance**: Empowering remote team members to manage their schedules and achieve work–life balance is essential for their well-being

and productivity. Leaders can offer flexible work hours, acknowledging different time zones and personal responsibilities. Promoting self-care and creating an environment that supports work–life integration contributes to higher employee satisfaction and engagement.

5. **Focus on results**: Successful remote team management revolves around a results-oriented focus—namely, focusing on outcomes rather than micromanaging processes. Trusting team members to deliver results encourages autonomy, fosters innovation, and allows individual strengths to shine. By focusing on results, leaders empower their remote teams to take ownership of their work and drive overall success.

CONCLUSION

If you have made it this far, I want to congratulate you on giving this topic the attention it deserves. By now, you should possess a deeper understanding of leadership than many so-called leaders out there. It is unfortunate that so many individuals in positions of power within organizations do not fully comprehend the extent of their influence over people. They mistakenly believe that their interactions with their team members only pertain to their professional lives, as if the two are separate entities. As presented in the Apple TV show "Severance," this misconception couldn't be further from the truth. Every interaction, whether positive or negative, resonates throughout every aspect of a person's life. Once we realize what power and influence we have and approach these with humility, empathy, and shared goals, our impact becomes infinite.

Now that you have journeyed through this book, you cannot unlearn what you have learned. You bear the responsibility of becoming a better leader. Even if you are already successful, consider dedicating yourself to one or two areas of improvement this year rather than spreading yourself too thin across all topics. Through deliberate practice to improve the skills you have, and extending the reach and range of your skills, you will reach heights within just a few years that few have ever attained.

Introspection is not an easy task. Looking inward and understanding our motives, the reasons behind our actions, and the emotions we experience can unveil uncomfortable memories, unresolved traumas, and deep-seated scars from the past. I have witnessed individuals breaking into tears during profound meditation sessions. However, the effort is worth it. The clarity, comfort, acceptance, and strength that come from embracing vulnerability will transform your personality and character.

The corporate world is in constant flux, presenting us with new challenges at every turn. No book, including this one, has all the answers. However, if you remain true to your authentic style, continue to learn and evolve, foster an open and safe culture for your team to provide feedback, embrace diverse perspectives and opinions, and, above all, prioritize the well-being of both you and your team, there is nothing you cannot overcome.

Allow me to leave you with the story that inspired me to write *The Corporate* and *Infinite Impact*. As you can tell from my bio, writing is not my primary profession.

Throughout my childhood, I observed the stress that overwhelmed my parents in their professional lives. I vividly recall the anxiety that consumed me whenever they received calls

CONCLUSION

from their bosses after working hours. Each day, I would anxiously await their return from work, assessing their stress level to figure out how I should behave around them. Unfortunately, this was the norm in most of my friends' households too. We discussed it a lot at school. I cannot imagine how my parents endured such toxic work cultures. Did their leaders ever consider the consequences of their actions? Were they aware that unrealistic expectations, long hours, and minimal rewards not only made life difficult for their employees but harmed their families, too?

Unfortunately, many of us could be that type of leader today. Unknowingly, you could be slowly breaking your subordinates and their families every single day. You may be kind and decent with strong values—except when you step into the workplace. And all the while, you may believe you are simply "doing your job." It's easy to exert authority over others when you possess positional power—you don't need emotional maturity to boss people around. After reading this book, I hope the evidence presented here has convinced you that there is a much better way to have a positive, infinite impact.

Today, you have the opportunity to choose what kind of leader you want to become and what legacy you wish to leave behind.

REFERENCES

Walker, M. (2017). Why We Sleep. Simon & Schuster.

Nestor, J. (2020). Breath: The New Science of a Lost Art. Riverhead Books.

Bradberry, T., & Greaves, J. (2009). Emotional Intelligence 2.0. TalentSmart.

Huberman Lab. https://open.spotify.com/show/79CkJF3UJTHFV8Dse3Oy0P?si=0946c12e05604a36

Bartlett, S. Diary of a CEO. https://open.spotify.com/show/7iQXmUT7XGuZSzAMjoNWlX?si=624b6d195b444de4

Huffington, A. (2017). The Sleep Revolution. Harmony.

Dweck, C. S. (2006). Mindset: The New Psychology Of Success. Ballantine Books.

Pink, D. H. (2018). When: The Scientific Secrets of Perfect Timing. Riverhead Books.

Pink, D. H. (2011). Drive: The Surprising Truth about What Motivates Us. Riverhead Books.

Nasr, A. (2021). The Corporate: The art of thriving in a competitive talent market

Dispenza, J. (2012). Becoming Supernatural: How Common People Are Doing the Uncommon.

Silva, J. (1978). The Silva Mind Control Method.

Attia, P., & Gifford, B. (2023). Outlive: The Science and Art of Longevity.

Harvard Business Review, Clear, J., Goleman, D., & Grant, H. (2022). HBR's 10 Must Reads on High Performance. Harvard Business Review Press.

Harvard Business Review, Drucker, P. F., Goleman, D., & George, B. (2011). HBR's 10 Must Reads on Leadership (with featured article "What Makes an Effective Executive," by Peter F. Drucker). Harvard Business Review Press.

Grenny, J., Patterson, K., McMillan, R., Switzler, A., & Gregory, E. (2023). Crucial Conversations: Tools for Talking When Stakes are High, Third Edition. McGraw-Hill Education.

Covey, S. M. R., & Merrill, R. R. (2008). The Speed Of Trust: The One Thing That Changes Everything. Free Press

Zhang, L., He, X., Ma, J., Liu, J., Xu, S., & Li, Y. (2020). Empathy, trust, and work engagement among public health nurses in China: A mediating role of affective commitment. *International Journal of Nursing Sciences, 7*(3), 318-326.

Hofstede, G. (2011). Dimensionalizing cultures: The Hofstede model in context. *Online Readings in Psychology and Culture, 2*(1), 1-26.

Blanchard, K. (2010). *The One Minute Manager.*

Covey, S. R. (2004). *The 7 Habits of Highly Effective People: Powerful Lessons in Personal Change.* Simon & Schuster.

Goleman, D. (2005). *Emotional Intelligence: Why it Can Matter More than IQ.* Bantam Books.

REFERENCES

Lencioni, P. (2012). *The Advantage: Why Organizational Health Trumps Everything Else in Business.* John Wiley & Sons.

Fernandez-Araoz, C. (2015). *It's Not the How or the What but the Who: Succeed by Surrounding Yourself with the Best.* Harvard Business Review Press.

Marquardt, M. J. (2012). *Building the Learning Organization: Achieving Strategic Advantage through a Commitment to Learning.* Nicholas Brealey Publishing.

Mintzberg, H. (2004). *Managers Not MBAs: A Hard Look at the Soft Practice of Managing and Management Development.* Berrett-Koehler Publishers.

Senge, P. M. (1990). *The Fifth Discipline: The Art and Practice of the Learning Organization.* Crown Business.

Schein, E. H. (2010). *Organizational Culture and Leadership.* John Wiley & Sons.

Kilmann, R. H., & Saxton, M. J. (2016). Toward a strategic theory of organizational culture. In *Handbook of Organizational Culture and Climate* (pp. 75-90). Routledge.

Cameron, K. S., & Quinn, R. E. (2011). *Diagnosing and Changing Organizational Culture: Based on the Competing Values Framework* (Vol. 1). John Wiley & Sons.

Goffee, R., & Jones, G. (2006). Managing authenticity: The paradox of great leadership. *Harvard Business Review, 84*(12), 88-96.

Denison, D. R., & Mishra, A. K. (1995). Toward a theory of organizational culture and effectiveness. *Organization Science, 6*(2), 204-223.

Kouzes, J. M., & Posner, B. Z. (2016). *The Leadership Challenge: How to Make Extraordinary Things Happen in Organizations.* John Wiley & Sons.

Armstrong, M. (2018). *Employee Reward Management and Practice: An Empirical Study in Ireland.* Routledge.

Edmondson, A. (1999). Psychological Safety and Learning Behavior in Work Teams. *Administrative Science Quarterly, 44*(2), 452-834.

Collins, J. (2001). *Good to Great: Why Some Companies Make the Leap... and Others Don't.* Harper Business.

Welch, J., & Welch, S. (2005). *Winning.*

Hamel, G. (2000). *Leading the Revolution: How to Thrive in Turbulent Times by Making Innovation a Way of Life.* Harvard Business Press.

Hackman, J. R., & Wageman, R. (2005). A Theory of Team Coaching. *Academy of Management Review, 30*(2), 269-287.

Zemke, R., Raines, C., & Filipczak, B. (2000). *Generations at Work: Managing the Clash of Veterans, Boomers, Xers, and Nexters in Your Workplace.* AMACOM.

Galinsky, E., & Bond, J. T. (2011). The 2008 National Study of the Changing Workforce. *Families and Work Institute.*

Neubert, M. J., Hunter, E. M., & Tolentino, R. C. (2016). A Servant Leader and Their Stakeholders: When Does Organizational Structure Enhance a Leader's Influence? *Journal of Business Ethics, 136*(4), 875-889.

AUTHOR BIO

Abdalla Nasr, author of the bestseller *The Corporate*, was born in Qatar and raised in the Middle East. He has worked across the Middle East, Africa, Asia Pacific, Europe, and the United States on multiple assignments to hire, assess, and develop talents at different organizational levels and to help business leaders with their people strategy, including building high-performing teams, transforming cultures, enhancing well-being and resilience, and improving productivity. He has received multiple awards for enabling businesses to achieve their goals by developing people leaders and building the right organizational culture. His bestselling book *The Corporate* has captured the interest and enthusiasm of readers keen to thrive in a competitive talent market.

For over a decade, and in more than 100 countries worldwide, because of his passion for people, culture, and well-being, Abdalla has striven to find the areas that employees and leaders could work on to improve productivity and reach their potential in the corporate world. Taking this keen interest a step further, he has interviewed leaders in the largest multinationals to get their views and opinions on how they view their talent.

He is passionate about helping people become the best version of themselves, personally and professionally. A fitness enthusiast, Abdalla takes every opportunity to travel and participate in outdoor activities and competitions.

Visit his website www.thecorporateofficial.com to learn more and connect with him.

Notes

Printed by BoD™in Norderstedt, Germany